Presentation Now

PEARSON

At Pearson, we take learning personally. Our courses and resources are available as books, online and via multi-lingual packages, helping people learn whatever, wherever and however they choose.

We work with leading authors to develop the strongest learning experiences, bringing cutting-edge thinking and best learning practice to a global market. We craft our print and digital resources to do more to help learners not only understand their content, but to see it in action and apply what they learn, whether studying or at work.

Pearson is the world's leading learning company. Our portfolio includes Penguin, Dorling Kindersley, the Financial Times and our educational business, Pearson International. We are also a leading provider of electronic learning programmes and of test development, processing and scoring services to educational institutions, corporations and professional bodies around the world.

Every day our work helps learning flourish, and wherever learning flourishes, so do people.

To learn more please visit us at: **www.pearson.com/uk**

Presentation Now

Prepare a perfect presentation in less than 3 hours

Andrew Lightheart

PEARSON

Harlow, England • London • New York • Boston • San Francisco • Toronto • Sydney
Auckland • Singapore • Hong Kong • Tokyo • Seoul • Taipei • New Delhi
Cape Town • São Paulo • Mexico City • Madrid • Amsterdam • Munich • Paris • Milan

Pearson Education Limited
Edinburgh Gate
Harlow CM20 2JE
United Kingdom
Tel: +44 (0)1279 623623
Web: www.pearson.com/uk

First published 2016 (print and electronic)

© Lightheart Workshops 2016 (print and electronic)

ISBN: 978–1-292–08145–8 (print)
        978–1-292–08147–2 (PDF)
        978–1-292–08148–9 (ePub)
        978–1-292–08146–5 (eText)

British Library Cataloguing-in-Publication Data
A catalogue record for the print edition is available from the British Library

Library of Congress Cataloging-in-Publication Data
Names: Lightheart, Andrew.
Title: Presentation now : prepare a perfect presentation in less than 3 hours
    / Andrew Lightheart.
Description: 1 Edition. | New York : Pearson, 2015. | Includes
    bibliographical references and index.
Identifiers: LCCN 2015038767 | ISBN 9781292081458 (pbk.)
Subjects: LCSH: Business presentations.
Classification: LCC HF5718.22 .L54 2015 | DDC 658.4/52--dc23
LC record available at http://lccn.loc.gov/2015038767

10 9 8 7 6 5 4 3 2 1
19 18 17 16 15

Illustrations by Bill Piggins
Cover design by Two Associates
Cover image © darsi/Shutterstock

Print edition typeset in 9.5/12.5pt Scene Std by 35
Print edition printed in Great Britain by Henry Ling Ltd, at the Dorset Press, Dorchester, Dorset

NOTE THAT ANY PAGE CROSS REFERENCES REFER TO THE PRINT EDITION

Contents

PART 3

EXTEND

For my husband Stuart.
With all my love.

About the author

Andrew Lightheart is a business communication specialist with extensive international experience in team dynamics, collaboration, conflict management, negotiation and leadership. Since the mid-1990s, he's been helping individuals and organisations radically optimise their spoken communication, including coaching 5,000 presentations by speakers hailing from 22 different countries.

He has assisted businesses from one-person micro-businesses, social enterprises and high-growth tech and law SMEs, through to HSBC (in UK, Hong Kong and China), GlaxoSmithKline, Siemens, Bank of America Merrill Lynch, and even 10 Downing Street.

After five years running a business in Asia, Andrew is proudly based at the Impact Hub in Birmingham, UK, a community of purpose-driven entrepreneurs, but travels globally to deliver talks, workshops and projects in English, Spanish, German and British Sign Language.

Andrew seeks out opportunities to support people from under-represented groups, particularly women and non-binary folk from BAME, LGBTQIA+ and Disabled communities. He believes that business (and life) is better when we can all stand up and speak up.

Acknowledgements

Saying thanks on completing your first book is really saying thanks for the people who've made the life you have that means you can *write* that book.

I'd like to thank, in vaguely chronological order:

My parents, Jenny Joy and John Cummings, for raising me to believe I could do anything I turned my hand to. Madeleine L'Engle, for making me want to fight for more light in the world, and for keeping me company through a lonely childhood.

Leahn Sharman and Emma Cole, for being my first flatmates and indirectly introducing me to my first training job. Claire Roche, for letting me come and be part of (and quickly become) the internal training department. Michael Breen, for teaching me to see and hear. Amanda Hughes, for taking a huge risk and giving me my first contract.

Ed Percival, for helping me to trust in my perspective. Karen Kingston, for connecting me.

Mike Sinnett and Fergie Williams, for bringing me into the bank. Havi Brooks, Naomi Dunford and Dave Navarro, for saving my business more times than I can count.

Shannon Casey, for sobriety and constancy. Andrea Henseler, for holding and supporting.

Helen Wood for still being there after all these years.

My mum-in-law Val Newberry, for the 'Caravan Office' years. Ness Cole and The Wolves, for bringing us to Birmingham. Rachel Donath for a meeting of minds.

Michelle Rayner, Naomi Watts and all at e4f, for being there at the birth of the book.

Immy Kaur and my Impact Hub Brum family, for supporting me in ways I could only dream of.

Eloise Cook, Lisa Robinson and Laura Blake at Pearson, for their belief and patience.

All my hundreds of clients from all over the world, who have taught me everything I know about presentations. My Twitter people, who've been (sometimes my only) friends. My nanny, Joyce Bull, for constant love. Samuel Sagan, for being my teacher.

Most of all, of course, I thank Stuart: my partner, witness, support, harbour, best friend, lobster and love of my life.

If this book has helped you, it's down to #teamlightheart.

Next week's big presentation

The way you've learned to prepare for presentations is traumatic and time-consuming. This book shows you how to plan efficiently, calmly and in your own style.

I'm assuming that:

- You've got a big presentation coming up.
- You're not a professional speaker.
- Presentations aren't your favourite thing.
- You want to do more than survive the experience.
- You have other priorities and don't want the planning to take over your life.
- You'd like to come across as calm, credible and engaging.

This book is the distillation of more than a decade's worth of my experience in helping technically-minded people become confident and compelling presenters.

I'll take you through a process which will get you from zero to a tailored, do-able presentation in less than three hours.

If you have additional time, you can work through a programme of quick wins and next steps designed to systematically lower your nerves, improve your delivery skills and help you create useful interaction after your presentation. Online chapters are available to take each skill further.

There are also tips for presenting in conference calls and speaking to international groups, plus a pep talk to read just before and just after your presentation.

A perfect presentation isn't a flawless 'performance'. A perfect presentation is one where you feel like you've done your best to achieve your aims. This book will help you do that in the most efficient and natural way possible.

How to use this book

This book is organised into three parts.

Part 1: PLAN takes you through a process to plan a specific presentation.

Part 2: SPEAK helps you with five aspects of how to deliver that presentation better.

You'll get significantly more benefit if you work through Part 1 before moving to Part 2.

Success is not guaranteed, but if you move systematically through these steps you'll know how to be much more in control of your situation.

Part 3: EXTEND takes your skills further into conference calls, international situations and ends with pep talks to give you confidence just before and just after doing any presentation.

You do not need a personality overhaul to be a significantly better presenter. This process is not going to break what's already working for you, but will build on your current skills and knowledge. All you have to do is relax and follow instructions. Presentations are about to get a whole lot easier.

PART 1
PLAN

Practical things

First off, we need to talk about practical things. You're going to need to get yourself in the right headspace. We'll be giving you a huge amount of traction on planning in just half an hour, but before that you need to get your kit ready and your head together.

Getting your kit ready

Let's start with the easiest part – your kit. Using the planning questions is a cyclical process: we'll do our first pass now, then later you might do a second and a third.

Decide how to record your ideas, so you can keep them clear for when you come back to them. Here are four options:

1. Worksheet people – if you like the idea of going through worksheets, head to **andrewlightheart.com/presentationnow** and print out the planning worksheets for this chapter. You'll be able to use them now, and then later in the planning process when you'll want to return to them.

2. Typing people – if you're more of a typing person, open five text documents. Save them as:
   - Who
   - Action
   - Past and present
   - Important
   - Plan.

3. Big paper people – if you prefer a bigger canvas to work on, grab an A3 pad and make a sheet for each of the five topics

above. If you're a mind mapper, use them as the central hubs for separate mind maps for each topic.

4. Other – if you prefer doing something else – for example, tiny notebooks, notes, walking and recording audio, whatever you like – get yourself sorted. I like the big paper option, Blu-tacked to the wall. I've been a flipchart-using facilitator for 20 years, so I think best on vertical spaces!

> **! WARNING!**
>
> It can be tempting to use the pre-preparation phase to avoid actual preparation. If you find yourself putting off the planning until you've gone to the stationery store, or find it really important to search online for exact instructions for mind maps on the internet, buy a book, obsess over specific pen colours or even suddenly think that it would be good to tidy and vacuum first . . . you're procrastinating!
>
> Print out the worksheets, or just get five sheets of paper out of the printer tray and start.

Timer – You'll need a timer: the clock app on your smartphone is perfect, or if push comes to shove, a clock. Following the time limits given is really important at this phase in the planning.

Getting your head together

Nothing you're about to learn is necessarily earth-shatteringly new, but this may be the first time that you have gone through these questions in this order (unless you're returning to this session for a subsequent time – in which case, welcome back!)

As with any new skill, allow the process to be clunky at first. Lower your expectations of how detailed your answers 'should' be, or how easily they 'should' flow. The idea is to get some forward motion.

Prepare yourself: make sure you've drunk enough water, had your usual amount of caffeine and eaten enough. Make sure you're in an environment that, if not perfect, at least doesn't totally wreck your concentration. For example, I like a bit of noise around me, so I work in a cafe, but my husband needs complete silence and solitude. Everyone is different. If you're a hermit, be a hermit. If you need surroundings that help your brain feel like it isn't missing out, head to the local cafe.

Ready? Okay – let's go!

1.
Get traction on planning
(30 minutes): Step 1

The whole process of presentation planning can be so overwhelming, partially because we start by asking ourselves the wrong first question (more about that in a minute). Follow the instructions in this chapter and you'll make a significant dent in your planning in just 30 minutes.

Over the past 10 years, working with speakers all over the world, I have come up with four questions. These four questions are where you start your planning process. They're also what you keep coming back to while you're planning, and where you turn when you get stuck. If you ever have coaching with me, we move through the planning process in the same way.

So many concerns you might have about presentation planning – such as how many slides you should use, whether you should move around or stand still, whether it's best to allow people to ask questions all the way through your talk, or get them to keep them until the end – are made much easier when you think properly about the situation you're going into. Essentially, the planning questions you're about to become familiar with will help you to be your own presentation coach.

Using these questions to think things through is going to make you a smarter and sexier presenter. It won't be a radical or difficult type of thinking; just pointing your brain in the right direction.

It hurts my heart when I see people who are super-smart in conversation become weird when they stand up in front of a group. Using these planning questions will help you not to be weird when you present, and will remove a whole lot of uncertainty about your presentation. What to say and how to say it will become, if not obvious, then at least more straightforward.

First, let's set the context for the questions you're going to answer by thinking about where *not* to start.

Don't start with this question

The wrong question to start planning your presentation with is: 'What will I say?'

It may seem the obvious place to start, what with you about to go and stand in front of people and say things, but it's the starting point of every poor presentation. There are no boundaries or scope to the answer, just the huge, amorphous field of Everything You Know. Speakers do strange things, speak in weird patterns and at the wrong level of detail because they haven't thought about the situation in which they find themselves.

We need to make sure that you prepare at the right level of detail, with a clear focus, so that you can plan rapidly, and that what you come up with is interesting, persuasive and do-able.

Here are the four questions to think about before you even begin to think about what to say.

Planning Question 1: what do I know about the people I'm talking to? (5 minutes)

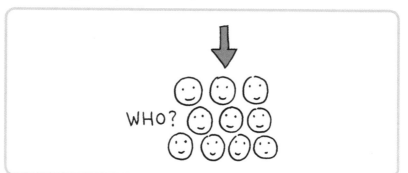

This is the best first question. By 'what do I know' I don't mean their preferences and inner life, but:

- their occupations
- their national culture
- their ages
- the basics.

You will find that some subgroups pop out. People often say, 'But my group is really mixed.' Without getting philosophical – not yet anyway, wait until we come around to these questions for the second and third time – every group is a mixed group. Hell, every individual is a mixed individual. The perennial problem of 'the mixed group' will be dealt with in detail later (see Chapter 2). For now, notice that there are certain ways in which people in your group differ from each other, and certain things that they have in common.

There are deeper benefits (for you) of thinking about the people you're going to be talking to, but all we're doing right now is getting some initial traction on the planning process.

IF YOU HAVE NO IDEA WHO YOU'LL BE TALKING TO

Sometimes you have no idea who's going to be in the room – or rather it feels like you don't. When someone gets me in to speak at an event, the whole room is full of strangers: it could be intimidating.

However, I can make a good guess at who will be there. For example, if a law firm wants me to speak to its staff, I can

➜

guess that they are probably going to be lawyers or support staff who work in the firm. Therefore, they are likely to be between 18 and 70, with the majority between 25 and 55. If the firm is in the United Kingdom, they are likely to speak fluent English and, if they practise UK law, they are likely to have been in the United Kingdom for a while.

In the same way, what can you guess about the people you will be talking to? Think about the possibilities. Rather than 'What do I know . . . ?', perhaps a better question is: 'What can I guess about the people I'm going to be talking to?' At this point in your planning process, the most general of generalities is fine. Two or three subgroups, with a bit of detail, is totally okay.

Planning Question 2: what do I want these people to be able and motivated to do after my presentation? (5 minutes)

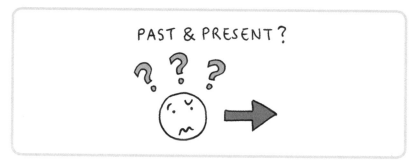

When I ask people something like 'Tell me about your presentation', after a great deal of backstory they start talking about 'key messages', or 'What they need to know is . . .'.

'Message thinking' is dangerous, and you'll find it all over the place. 'Decide on your key message', they say, 'What are the major takeaways?' If you're overly detailed or go off on a tangent easily, it's good to be focused and precise.

However, message thinking is still focused on *you* – and the point of your presentation has nothing to do with you.

The point of the presentation is all about them.

This question is your compass. It will help you filter your information so you can pitch it in simple terms and at the right level.

Let's look at the component parts of the question.

These people

Your presentation is specifically for the people you're talking to. If you ever do a roadshow where you take the same presentation from place to place, you *must* rethink it each time for the people who are going to be there on that occasion. The major mistake reported back to me from people attending this kind of presentation is that they felt processed on a conveyor belt, talked at with irrelevant content, and that it would have made no difference if they were physically there listening or not.

The more you can make your presentation tailored to the specific people you're talking to, the easier everything else falls into place.

Do

What action do you want these people to take:

- during the presentation
- immediately afterwards
- that day
- the next day
- next week
- next month?

Be as specific as you can, but don't get hung up on details right now. We need to be keeping things moving.

Be wary of words such as 'understand' and 'buy-in'. Think: if your presentation is successful, what would these people be doing differently?

One way of moving from a concept to an action is to add: 'so that they . . .' to the end of the sentence. For example, 'I want people to buy in . . .':

'I want people to buy in *so that they* . . .' – sign off, discuss positively, agree to another meeting?

'I want people to understand these concepts *so that they...*' –
stop doing something, start doing something, change the way
they do something?

Able

There are two aspects to people taking any recommended action.
First, check that your recommendation is an action that these
people are able to take. What resources might they need in order to
follow your suggestion? (Hint: time, money, ability, knowledge, skills.)

If they are lacking any of these resources sufficiently, then they
can't take your recommended action.

Motivated

Secondly, do they want to take that action? Or, if they are unlikely
to *want* to, are they required to do it by something else in their
environment? Are they motivated to take that action? Can you
motivate them more?

ABLE AND MOTIVATED: TWO ASPECTS

I arrived in my hotel room in Hong Kong a few months ago.
I often work in Hong Kong and the client gets a special deal at
this hotel – so much so that we get a club room, which means
that we can use the club lounge. We could never afford this
ourselves, so it's a really nice perk. After we'd been in the room
a couple of minutes, the phone rang. It was the club lounge,
asking if we wanted to upgrade to a suite.

The poor chap on the phone launched into his spiel about
all the benefits of a suite (that he was reading off a list) and,
yes, it sounded lovely. I genuinely wanted to upgrade. Sure!
Why not?

So I *wanted* it – but I wasn't *able* to. Why? We don't book our
accommodation – the client does. So no matter how enticing
he made his recommendation, no matter how wonderful it was or
how badly I wanted to take him up on the offer, I wasn't *able* to.

So, two parts: able and motivated.

If your listeners are clearly *not able* to follow your recommendation or request, it's good to know that now. Also, if they're going to need a lot of motivating, it helps to see that from the beginning of your planning too.

EXERCISE

Set your timer for 5 minutes. Stare into the distance and write some ideas for possible actions that you might want these people to take during, just after, a little bit after and a lot after your presentation.

If you find yourself thinking in abstract terms about 'understanding' or 'buy-in', ask yourself: 'What would I see or hear if that was happening?' When the timer goes, stop.

Planning Question 3: what can I guess about their past and present? (10 minutes)

In your mind, choose a member of the group you're talking to: imagine walking up to them cold and asking them to take the action you're recommending.

Straight away, what questions would they have? What objections, concerns, thoughts, feelings, attitudes or prejudices would move them towards or away from doing it right away?

You know that phrase 'the elephant in the room'? The huge thing that for some reason remains unspoken? I was working with an IT leader for a multinational bank that was in the middle of a huge round of unwanted redundancies. He was

➜

presenting at a roadshow about the department's plan for the next six months.

You know what the elephant in the room would be? The 'redundancy elephant'. It's as if there were an enormous, hairy elephant in the room with 'Redundancy' sprayed on its side, with the speaker not mentioning it.

Everyone in the room would be turning to their neighbour, saying, 'Er . . . you see that elephant, right?' – and while doing that, they wouldn't be able to concentrate on anything else.

I advised that guy to phone the human resources director, find out what he could say and what he couldn't, and start the presentation with that information. Then, as he started talking about the rest of his plan, people could settle down because at least they knew he had told them everything he was able to about the redundancies.

You have to name the elephants that you know are going to be in people's minds: if you can't get them out of the room, at least move them to one side so people can hear what you're saying.

It's more than elephants

So, you need to name, acknowledge and deal with the elephants – but really 'elephants' is understating it. If you could look inside the heads of your listeners, you wouldn't find just elephants. It's a freaking circus in there. There are trapeze artists, and clowns, and acrobats, and tightrope walkers, and a brass band. Lions and tigers and bears, oh my.

During all the time that you'll be speaking to them, your listeners are full of thoughts, feelings and silent questions – and not just about you and your topic, but their whole life. The idea that they're just sitting there, blank and ready to hear your message, is a ridiculous fantasy. It's also important not to think they are totally focused on you and hate you with all of their might (there is more about the horror movies we create in Chapter 7: Calm).

Planning Question 4: what is important to them? (5 minutes)

What do your listeners need and want? What do they need and want urgently? What do they value?

I see technical people fall down most when they don't frame things in terms that are important and understandable to their listeners. The feedback I get from the non-technical side of an organisation is that the technical side 'doesn't speak our language'.

It's partially what is called the 'problem of knowledge': you know so much about your topic that it's difficult to climb inside the mind of someone who, by comparison, knows nothing or next to nothing about it.

When you talk about things purely from your point of view, you become boring. People get restless and interrupt, or give a bland response and you never hear from them again.

This is a vitally important question for fairly high-level philosophical reasons; however, right now we're going to look at it for nitty-gritty purposes.

In connection to your topic, what do these people need and want? What are their preferences?

How does your suggestion or request help them to move closer to achieving their priorities?

Here's a thought experiment: think about phone apps. If you're at all literate in how things are coded, think about how much work, how many thousands of hours have gone into putting that app onto the market. I've sat next to my friend Carl as he put together an app. It's intense work, every step to get a click on a button to lead onto the next screen, then save the data in the background: it's a full-on task. To put together an app that people will pay for and rely on is a major undertaking, often needing a huge team.

On your smartphone (or just the Internet), go to an app store. Look at a big, popular, paid app: a business one. Look at something like an accounting app, or something that backs up notes.

Read the description of the app.

How much technical detail is there? How much description is there about the language it's written in, the database architecture it rests on, the iterations it went through to get to be at all reliable? None, right? So, let's think this through.

What is important to the users of an app that is going to back up and hold all their notes:

- Is it reliable?
- No, really. Is it reliable?

- Can I edit the notes easily?
- Can I find my notes easily?
- Is there a word limit?
- Can I access them on any device?
- Can I type in my own language?
- Can I send email to it?
- Oh, and how much does it cost?

These are all functional concerns that must be addressed. Does anyone care or even think about what language it's built in, where the headquarters are, how long it was in development or how much it is staying up-to-date with current standards? No.

I worked with a big pharmaceutical company in Switzerland. It was doing a launch of a drug trial where it wanted to get doctors to sign up specific patients in a particular timescale. The company brought me in to help with its presentations.

I was working with the lead scientist. She got out her slides and started talking. 'Five years ago . . . Then we . . . Then we . . .' She wanted to tell the whole story: it was important to her – it was five years of her life! But would the doctors care? Would knowing all the details of the iterations of the testing and the progress of the project move the doctors closer to signing up or further away?

What do you think was important to the doctors:

- Is the drug safe?
- Who specifically is it good for?
- Will being part of this study build my professional reputation?
- What's in the goody bag?
- What's for lunch?

(Unfortunately, young coach that I was, I didn't manage to wrest her History Of The Project slides away from her. Things would be different these days, believe me.)

What does this mean? Think through the lives of your listeners. In those subgroups, what is important to them in their jobs? In their daily lives, what are their priorities? If you don't know, go and do five minutes of searching online.

In Step 2 we're going to think this through, but for now, some general ideas will help you begin to filter your content.

HINT: WHAT TO DO IF RIGHT NOW YOU ARE FROZEN IN PANIC

If you can't get moving at all on this, then go back to Question 1 and halve all the timings. Do it on a piece of paper, try not to judge or edit as you're going along. You're going to come back to your notes and it's all likely to change anyway. This is just serving the purpose of getting you unstuck. You'll get you through this, I promise. Just relax and follow instructions.

Planning Question 5: what is immediately apparent to you now? (5 minutes)

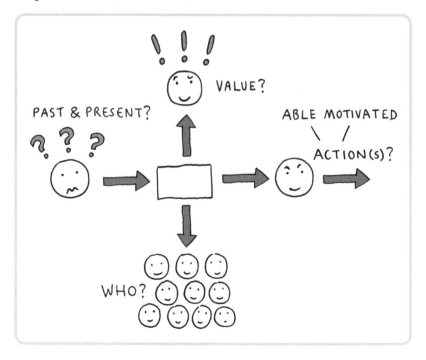

Get your notes together and look through them again:

1. **What do I know about the people I'm talking to?** Look at what you know about the people you're going to be talking to. Even having spent five minutes thinking about this question has already put you head and shoulders above the 'what will I talk about?' crowd.

2. **What do I want these people to be able and motivated to do after my presentation?** Review your outcomes. Are they still reasonable and probable, bearing in mind the answers to the other planning questions? The responses you would like them to have become your compass and filter for your content. You'll keep coming back to them (and refine them as you go).

3. **What can I guess about their past and present?** Go over again what silent questions they have, and what could be going on in their internal circus. These are the things you're going to have to deal with, if you want them to begin moving towards your outcome.

4. **What is important to them?** Finally, get a feel for what's really important to them. How can you show them that following your request is going to get them more of what they want, need and value?

What is immediately obvious? What do you absolutely have to include in your presentation? What, more importantly, do you need to leave out?

Make brief notes.

Seriously, well done! You've taken better steps towards an effective presentation in the past half an hour than most speakers ever take. This will take a good 10 per cent edge off your overwhelm. Now you have a place to start: feels better, right?

Okay, time to let that settle. Take a break, do something different for a bit. Go for a walk, look out the window, do some star jumps or something. Eat, drink, breathe in and out.

The next step is to return to the questions and refine your answers.

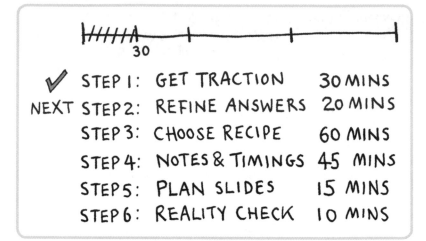

✔	STEP 1:	GET TRACTION	30 MINS
NEXT	STEP 2:	REFINE ANSWERS	20 MINS
	STEP 3:	CHOOSE RECIPE	60 MINS
	STEP 4:	NOTES & TIMINGS	45 MINS
	STEP 5:	PLAN SLIDES	15 MINS
	STEP 6:	REALITY CHECK	10 MINS

2.
Refine your answers
(20 minutes): Step 2

Now you've gone through the questions once and let them settle, it's time to return and refine your answers.

List subgroups (5 minutes)

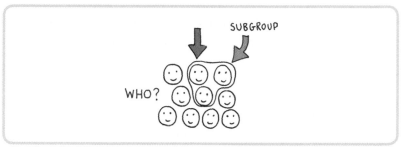

If your group is larger than, say, 10 people, one thing that will pop out straight away is that you don't have just one group in front of you; you have multiple subgroups. For example, if you're a lawyer doing a briefing on the Construction Act, you might have architects, facilities managers and builders in your group. If you're talking to a wider IT department, you might have some people from production support, some from IT architecture, some from User Experience and some from testing.

You are not a homogenous person

When you find yourself thinking about a group as one homogenous mass, it's a sign that you'll need to be extra vigilant. I mean, I'm not even a homogenous person. Are you?

Think about all the roles you play in your life:

Who are you in your job? What is your job title? Your seniority? Your experience? Where are you based?

What about outside of work: what groups could you legitimately join?

How else could someone categorise you: by preference for technology, education, gender, national culture, religious or non-religious affiliation?

Are you a parent? If so, what kind of parent?

Do you follow certain food preferences? Are you allergic to something? Are you a gourmet?

What about hobbies?

What do you feel strongly about?

Do you have a car? What type of car? Do you care?

Are you a Mac user? A superfan, or just because it's easy? Hardcore Linux installer? Plain out-of-the-box Windows user?

What kind of books do you read? How about films?

Do you care about the environment? Are you a believer in recycling?

Where do you get your news from?

Which social media tools do you use?

Are you cats, dogs, iguanas or none or the above?

Morning or evening person?

Are you outdoorsy or inside-good?

Do you track everything financially, go with the flow or just monitor your budget?

Now take that to 10, 100, 1000 members of your group. You have to make peace with the fact that your group is a mixed group on every level. So in the end, we have to go with general trends, but keep in mind the complexity of human experience.

EXERCISE

Set your timer for 5 minutes. If your group has more than eight people in it, spend 5 minutes listing the subgroups that are in your group. If your group has fewer than about eight people and you know each person, list the individuals.

Develop a range of outcomes (5 minutes)

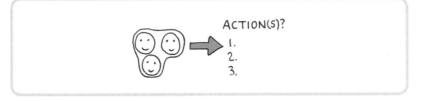

Do you secretly think it's going to take a miracle to get the people in your group to follow your recommendations? Don't be scared to list a range of outcomes – from absolute minimum to 'fist pump' – so you're ready to be flexible on the day. Bear in mind what is achievable with the time, people and skills that you have available to you. Very often on the day it will turn out that you have less than your originally allotted time, so it's sensible to plan for what to do if that happens.

Your outcomes affect the rest of your planning process, so do your best to choose them realistically.

Remember to include what you want to happen both during and after your presentation:

Do you want discussion to happen? If so, what type and when?

Do you have different actions you'd like different subgroups to take? This is the time to think about them.

Think through the past and present for subgroups (5 minutes)

Select one of the subgroups you've identified: perhaps the one that has the most contribution or importance to your outcome. List all the questions, concerns, attitudes and prejudices that they're going to be bringing with them.

Select another subgroup. What else do they bring with them that is different to the first subgroup?

You really can't do too much of this, so if you have time, do more. Think where they might get confused, and what misconceptions they might have about your topic that you can correct.

Think about values for important subgroups (5 minutes)

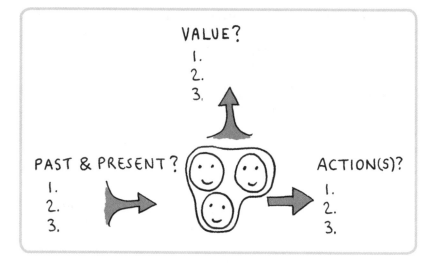

Ask yourself: what is important to the subgroups in this group? What are their priorities?

Also, what do you think they'll need and want from you *in this context*?

As you turn to select which recipe to use for your presentation, you'll find that you need to link your content to benefits. The more you put yourself in the shoes of the people listening, the easier this will be.

Now you've spent significant time thinking about the people you're going to talk to, it's finally time to begin to think about what you're going to say, and how you're going to say it.

The next step is to get familiar with the ingredients of effective presentations and what combinations of ingredients will work for your situation.

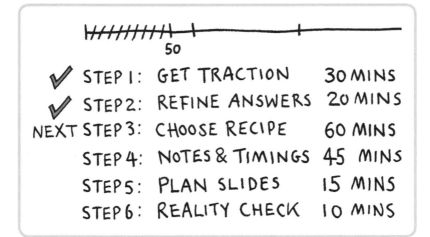

STEP 1: GET TRACTION — 30 MINS
STEP 2: REFINE ANSWERS — 20 MINS
NEXT STEP 3: CHOOSE RECIPE — 60 MINS
STEP 4: NOTES & TIMINGS — 45 MINS
STEP 5: PLAN SLIDES — 15 MINS
STEP 6: REALITY CHECK — 10 MINS

3.
Select an appropriate presentation recipe (60 minutes): Step 3

Ingredients

When I watch presentations, I see certain things happening again and again. In this chapter we will look at each of these ingredients, their importance and how you can use them. In the second half of this chapter, we look at how those ingredients form recipes.

When you're learning a skill, it can be useful to have a lens to look through. When I am cooking a new recipe, I tend to make it the first time exactly as it's written. Then when I get a feel for it, I'll experiment. When you know your ingredients or a process, you can approach a recipe in a different way. For example, I make a lot of bread by hand, and when I look at a bread recipe I can run it through in my mind and see if it's going to be a wet dough, or if it's going to need more time to rise.

The presentation recipes here are just starting points. Starting from a blank page can be hard, so they will point you in the right direction. Adapt them to match your situation!

Below are ingredients for you to work with: these are the significant aspects that need to be thought through and that are not difficult to include, even if you're not very experienced or haven't got much time to practise. You can incorporate them without too much effort, and they will almost certainly improve your presentation.

Benefits and downsides

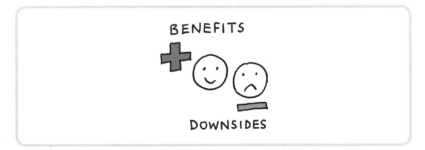

When I'm coaching corporate IT people who need to present to business people, it can seem like they are speaking in a different language, with different priorities. So much so that the businesspeople end up feeling that IT don't speak *their* language. It's the same with lawyers talking to non-lawyers, finance people speaking to non-finance people and so on.

Speaking the language of your listeners needn't be about using jargon. It's more about framing things in terms that are relevant – and relevance is key to being interesting.

People can't skim through your talk like they can do with a document, so you need to get their interest and keep it. One major way you can do this is by making clear what the benefits and downsides of your recommendations are, in terms they can relate to.

The benefits

The benefits are the reasons why people should listen to you. They are what can be gained by following your recommendations.

The downsides

The downsides are what your listeners stand to lose if they don't follow your recommendation. More often we are motivated to take action by what we stand to lose, rather than by what we stand to gain. In fact, if you are recommending a change to the status quo, you have to make that change less painful than the pain of staying the same. Why? Because even if people hate the status quo, they'll still prefer it to having to change.

In addition to finding clear reasons why following your recommendation will make their life better, you'll be even more persuasive if you can find reasons why staying the same will mean that they might lose what's important to them.

A lawyer briefing their clients about the importance of keeping contemporaneous notes is up against quite a bit of status quo love.

Keeping notes is a pain, especially for people who avoid paperwork: it's extra work. They might feel like their handwriting

➡

won't be good enough, so they'll need to type up their notes; or they're not sure about how detailed to make them. If they have never had to refer to notes, they won't see any danger in staying the same as they are: i.e. not taking notes.

To effect change, it might be useful for the lawyer to tell their clients some warning stories about the consequences of not having notes: a client who was sued because they didn't have evidence of what was said in a meeting, for example. The size of the case and the repercussions for them would need to be made apparent.

It is important to make those downsides clear.

Also, the lawyer should make the **benefits** clear. What are the benefits of keeping notes? Well, *not* being sued, obviously, but also peace of mind and professionalism. An unexpected benefit is being able to refer back to them before the client has a subsequent meeting, and being much more able to track activity and workload.

Introducing benefits and downsides into the recipe

The best way to do this is to make clear at the start of your presentation what the group is going to get by listening to you, and what the downsides of not listening are. At the end, reiterate those benefits and downsides.

Then as you introduce each point, do this again. Tell them why listening to this point will give them more of what they want, and how missing it out will mean they'll lose what's important to them.

Evidence

People are not in the habit of following the advice of just any pretty stranger. If you're making a point, you need to support it with evidence, which can take many forms. We're going to discuss a key form of evidence below: story (which is so fundamental we will be dealing with it in Chapter 10). Other types of evidence can include:

- statistics
- facts
- scenarios
- appeals to other authority
- demonstration.

Some evidence has more emotional impact, and some has a more rational impact. Think: 'With what I know or can guess about these people, what do they need to hear and evaluate to begin to accept my point?'

Story

Ah, story: the 'secret' that spoken communication relies on. When you want to grab people's attention, make a point more persuasive, show your experience, teach something valuable, warn people away from something or just make a point more vivid, story is your friend.

There are a lot of myths about story, including that you need to be some kind of born storyteller to do it well. This is rubbish. Telling stories in presentations is a learnable skill (which we'll find out more about in Chapter 10).

Think back through the life of the project you're discussing, and think what experiences you or your team (if you have one) have had to support your point. Here, you're looking for experiences that work as evidence. Think about stories that show benefits, and stories that warn people away from downsides. Think about problems you solved (or didn't solve, if you're issuing a warning).

Focus on four parts:

1. when, where and who
2. size of the problem or challenge
3. actions
4. result.

Forget about funny or interesting stories. Just think: evidence.

Signposting

Your listeners need to know where they are in the presentation when they listen to you. You need to strike a balance between too much signposting and too little.

Too much signposting

This leads to the phenomenon of spoilers. Think about how much you avoid information about a TV show you're watching or a movie you want to see, scared that you'll find out something that will spoil your enjoyment. (I'm not much for sports analogies, but I do remember my dad avoiding finding out the football score before he'd seen *Match of the Day*.)

Why do we care about spoilers so much? If we know what's coming up, on some level our mind shuts down because it feels like it's already happened. You have to be careful not to 'spoil' your presentation by telling people exactly what's coming up. Why? Because they will feel like they have already heard it. It becomes significantly more difficult to keep people's attention if you've killed their curiosity.

Too little signposting

However – and this is a big however – people don't like *not* knowing what's happening at all. For example, a while ago I went to see Stanley Kubrick's *2001: A Space Odyssey* on the big screen. The film starts on the savannah, and goes thus:

> Long scene of empty savannah.
>
> Long scene of monkeys grazing on savannah.
>
> Long scene of fighting off rival troupe of monkeys on savannah.
>
> Long scene of monkeys waking up to big, black obelisk standing in the savannah, with rousing music.

Kubrick, the director, really stretches your curiosity – almost to breaking point. But being totally lost? Watching a random series of images or a movie with a comedy scene, then a horror scene, then a landscape, then a period comedy . . . You'd soon lose patience.

Balancing signposting

In sum: if you do too much signposting, people find it hard to pay attention because they feel like they know what's coming up. If you don't give them enough signposting, it's hard for them to pay attention because they don't know what the heck is happening.

> Too much signposting = too much safety = boredom
>
> Too little signposting = too much uncertainty = confusion

Your job as a presenter is to balance safety with curiosity.

When we get to the recipes I'll be recommending a certain style of signposting depending on the demands of the situation, including your listeners' tolerance for uncertainty and propensity to boredom.

Just be aware that your style of signposting will depend a lot on who you're talking to, and what actions you want them to take.

Effective ways to strike a balance

Two effective ways you can strike this balance are with *signpost questions* and *curiosity keywords*.

To use signpost questions, take three to five big chunks of your presentation and think: 'What question does each chunk answer?'

Then, when you get to the point in your introduction when you're laying out what is about to happen, instead of telling people the areas, say: 'By the end of this session, you'll have the answer to five questions . . .' – and then list the questions.

People will know how many chunks there are in the presentation, so they'll feel safe, but they'll also stay curious.

Refer back to your answers to Planning Question 4 to make sure that the questions link to benefits they are interested in. **Curiosity keywords** need a bit of careful handling, but can work equally well. They are when you take the big sections of your presentation, and, instead of giving them straightforward keywords, find a keyword that doesn't immediately make sense, but will by the end of that chunk.

One of my favourites recently came from my marketing coach, who was giving a talk. She said, 'There are two reasons you leave writing content to the end of your website planning: burnout and broccoli.'

Huh? You know how many chunks there are, yet still remain curious.

SUBTLE SIGNPOSTING SKILLS

In fact, whenever you are listing something in your presentation – for example, reasons, benefits, features, techniques – at first just tell them how many elements there are and only explain them as you get to them. One way to so this is to simply say 'There are three main techniques you need to focus on when first approaching this tool. The first one is . . .'. Then only after explaining that first one do you say, 'The second one is . . .'. It's

→

---

also a good habit to introduce each topic with its place in the presentation and end with a summary: 'That was the second technique. The third one is . . .'. Sequence words such as 'First . . . secondly . . . finally' to help people to keep track. Emotional words such as 'surprisingly' and 'luckily' are ways to introduce a point by creating a bit of curiosity about the next sentence.

Setting boundaries

Disappointment is the feeling we get when our expectations are not met. We picture a situation and the reality doesn't match what we pictured. I've observed effective speakers using a particular phrase often enough for it to become a clear pattern. One way to avoid disappointing your listeners is to be really clear about what's going to be covered: what's in and what's out.

What's in and what's out

This one's very simple. Start every session with a statement about what is and is not going to be covered. For example: 'What I'm not going to be able to do today is . . .', 'What I am going to be able to do is . . .'.

In this way people will know they are in the right place, and will relax.

Setting boundaries like this is also a way to avoid awkward questions in the question and answer section of your presentation (Q&A). If there is a limit to your knowledge of a certain topic, you need to make that clear from the start; then you've got a get-out clause if someone wants to quiz you on something outside the scope of your talk later. For example: 'I'm afraid that's a bit outside what we're covering today.'

Silent questions

One mindshift that is really going to help you be more interesting is to plan your presentation by considering: 'What questions might my listeners have about this point?'

An important time you need to do this is at the beginning of your session. You've already done it to some extent by thinking through the silent questions that your listeners might have about you (and people like you), your topic and recommendations.

One of the first things to do at the start of your presentation is to answer the major silent questions people have – either overtly with words, or implicitly by your manner.

If, for example, people expect your topic to be complex and confusing, you can deal with that by overtly saying: 'I bet you think this is going to be complex and confusing, but let me tell you how things are going to be different today.' Or you can do it with your manner: you can 'answer' the question by using conversational language, being approachable and labelling the big chunks of your presentation in ordinary words that your listeners can understand.

As you move to each new point, you have to go through this process again.

Think:

As I bring up this point, what worries, concerns, objections, attitudes, prejudices or misconceptions might my listeners have?

What obstacles might get in the way of their listening in the first place, and subsequently moving in the direction I'd like them to?

If you do this well, people will really feel like you are interesting, because you're matching the thoughts going on in their mind. It feels like you're reading their mind. You want them thinking, 'That's just what I was thinking!'

Experience matching

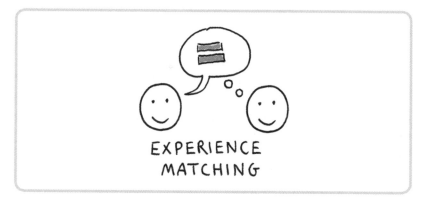

In a presentation, the way that you establish your credibility is not by listing your achievements, or by making a big deal of the projects you've worked on or the clients you have.

Credibility is established by matching your content to what your listeners are thinking. If what you say matches their understanding of the situation, you'll take down a barrier to their listening.

The people sitting in the room need reasons to listen to you. One of the things you don't want to do is to trigger 'otherness' in them. If you start off too differently from them in terms of energy level, jargon and technical expectations, you can jar them out of listening. Sure, a very skilled communicator can make an impact by doing something unexpected, but it's a risky strategy.

'Make an impact' is one of the phrases that you read a lot when you start looking into presentations, but it can just mean 'make a bad impression' – and often indicates a speaker's lack of confidence that they can be successful just by being themselves.

Go back to your answers to Planning Question 2: 'What do I want these people to be able and motivated to do after my presentation?' Making a true impact is measured by people taking action, not by you doing something that isn't genuine.

You need to provide your listeners with reasons to listen to you – both overtly and implicitly.

If you can:

- match what they are thinking
- describe their past situation and
- describe their current situation

– you will find that people are much more willing to listen to you, as you are someone who is obviously *worth* listening to.

Speak the language of their situation

Speak about what your listeners might be concerned about. Describe things that are current to them, or at least mention them.

Find out what they might be thinking

There are two ways to do this:

1. Go online and find out what the current issues are for their industry or department.
2. Ask them. If you know people who might be in the group, find out what they might be looking for in this session and what their concerns might be.

Notice that by describing their current situation, you are demonstrating your credibility by matching their experience. This, without tricks, builds trust – because you are showing that you understand their situation and care about it.

Ingredients summary

Now that you've looked at the ingredients:

- benefits and downsides
- evidence
- story
- signposting
- boundaries
- silent questions
- experience matching

– it's time to see how they combine into the right recipe for your situation.

Recipes

Here, I'm making the assumption that you don't want to become a professional speaker, or that this isn't your immediate aim. When I teach a presentation masterclass, my aim is to help participants to learn how to taste the 'ingredients' and learn how to 'cook'. There are almost no recipes in our classes, but you (a) don't have the time, money or opportunity to take our classes, and (b) need answers now. So I'm going to give you some recipes.

The following cover the majority of situations that you'll be going into: each one includes a description of when it's useful, and some warnings or guidance. Choose the one that most closely matches your situation.

 WARNING!

Don't try and use the recipes in this section if you haven't gone through the previous planning steps. If you've skipped straight here, go back to Chapter 1 and think about who your listeners are! Cooking a recipe without knowing who's going to be eating it is a disaster (or at least a damp squib) waiting to happen. This won't take long, and it will make the process of using the recipes much smoother. Being tuned into your listeners is essential to making smart adjustments for your particular situation.

Choose your recipe

SENIOR PITCH

For when you have a project, recommendation or proposal that needs approval or sign-off to move forward.

CONFERENCES

For events where you're doing what we might think of as a conventional talk.

SPECIALIST BRIEFING

For when you're doing a briefing on your specialist topic to people who are specialists in your topic.

NON-SPECIALIST BRIEFING

For when you're doing a briefing on your specialist topic to people who aren't specialists in your topic.

PROJECT UPDATE

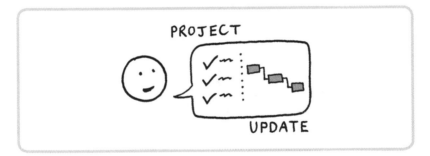

For when you're telling people about what's happened recently in your project.

BAD NEWS

For telling people bad news.

AWARENESS-RAISING

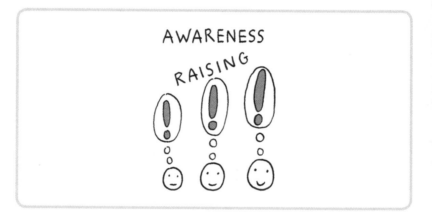

For when you've got a project or an idea and you want more people to know about it.

EXERCISE

Set your timer for 60 minutes. Choose your recipe and put an outline together.

1. Select the recipe that most closely represents your situation.

2. Lay out a possible sequence, just with keywords. Think of this as a sketch.

Senior pitch

When you have a project, recommendation or proposal that needs approval or sign-off to move forward.

Recipe

Part 1:

  Life without your recommendation

  Life with your recommendation

  Action

  Silent questions

Part 2:

  The whys

  The what-abouts.

Guidance

The senior pitch recipe is for when you're going into a group of people to get their sign-off on a plan and you have limited time.

It's important that you use your time very wisely in these situations. The reason that senior people often interrupt is because the wrong things are put upfront. Pitching to busy people is a skill, because you need to answer their silent questions very quickly – or they won't be able to stay silent for very long!

There are two parts to the senior pitch. The first is getting through their initial gatekeeping.

Senior people hear a lot of pitches, so they sort for rejection rather than inclusion. If you've ever sorted CVs, you'll be familiar with this.

Initially, at least, you don't look for reasons to *include* people on your shortlist, you look for reasons to sort them *out*. This first section of your presentation lasts maybe two or three minutes and needs careful planning. If you can do this well, you earn the right to keep talking.

The second is a flexible set of answers to questions they may ask. You've got to be ready for the obvious questions they are going to ask, and the non-obvious ones too. It may be that you deliver this information in the form of a presentation, or more of a Q&A session.

DISCOURAGE INTERRUPTIONS
Very often, people tell me that their boss doesn't let them get through their presentation, but interrupts almost immediately. When someone tells me this, I ask: 'When would you interrupt someone? If someone junior (or unfamiliar) to you came to do a presentation, when would you feel compelled to interrupt?' The answer to this is often: 'Well, if I felt like my time was being wasted. Or if I wasn't clear what the purpose or relevance of the presentation was.' What I hear from senior people is: 'I just want people to say what they want.'

DON'T BE A 'CHUGGER'
If you're not careful, suddenly you're in the position of one of those 'chuggers': charity muggers. You know, the ones who accost you in the street, all friendly, energetic and perky when you're just trying to get from A to B?

To stop your presentation from feeling like this, you have to think about it purely from the perspective of your listeners. When a chugger approaches you, there is nothing in it for you. It feels like an ambush. This doesn't mean that it's a bad charity, or that donating isn't worthy and good. It's just that there is – on the surface at least – nothing in it for you, and everything in it for the person doing the asking.

VALUE THE RELATIONSHIP
When you are pitching an idea or project, you probably want a sustained relationship with the people you're pitching to. If you 'trick' them, you'll only be able to do it once and never again.

The secret to making your pitch work is to think about it from your listeners' perspective, and talk about it only in terms of the impact it has on the things they care about.

I was coaching a senior manager who looks after a team of 3,000 IT engineers. She had to propose a change to the way that a particular project was being approached. When I asked her why it was important, she said it had to do with the purity of the IT architecture: there were certain efficient principles that the project wasn't following, and it just wasn't right. Fair enough – but the project was already one-third completed, so there were issues of momentum and sunk costs.

When I asked who she was going to be pitching to, it was to managers from the business side of her organisation. I asked her the four planning questions, including: 'What's important to these people?' What was important was revenue, profit, a quiet life, reputation and not creating more work for themselves or their team. What was not important to them was purity of IT architecture principles. All they cared about was how it impacted on them. Once she got that straight, planning became simpler.

MAKE YOUR PITCH INCREDIBLY TAILORED

Unless people can see that your recommendation is clearly going to *give* them more of what they need and value, and the *costs* of changing are much less than the costs of another option (or staying the same), they are not going to go with it.

If budget is an issue, then you have to be able to show actual financial amounts for how your solution will cost less than the other solution. Also, that it will make their lives better in ways they care about.

In fact, try and pitch it by only mentioning things they naturally care about. If you have to do a bunch of explaining why your recommendation is a good thing, you may well lose them.

UNLESS IT'S A 'RUBBER STAMP' SITUATION

The only exception here is something that has no obvious alternatives, and costs your listeners nothing to approve. For example, if you want approval for a change in a process that has no impact on any of the people present (including little or no resistance from the other people in your department), you won't have to work so hard on relevance.

The more it affects the senior people's life in terms of budget, reputation or hassle, the clearer you have to make the benefits.

DON'T UNDERESTIMATE THE POWER OF SMALL STORIES
You don't have to be telling 'Save the World' stories to demonstrate a point. A small example or two can be very persuasive, especially if you make clear why the problem was important or urgent in that moment (for more advice on this, see Chapter 10).

Full recipe

PART 1

Life without your recommendation: match their experience by describing their current situation, including downsides that they can relate to (one or two sentences).

Life with your recommendation: describe how their life will be better after following your recommendation, with high-level benefits that they can relate to (one or two sentences).

Action: what you want them to do today. Just come out and say it.

Silent questions: answer their biggest silent questions, including:

- how what you're recommending could come about (process/ implementation)
- why your recommendation is a good thing
- why it's not going to be a hassle or risk for them (or why the hassle or risk is worth it).

PART 2

Be ready either to include these as part of your presentation, or have them ready as responses to spoken questions.

The whys:

- Why you and not someone else?
- Why this and not something else?
- Why that much and not less (or more)?
- Why now and not later (or before)?
- Why this way and not another way?

The what-abouts – what-abouts are bespoke, but include:

- What about that thing that happened before?
- What about that thing people are saying?
- What about the fact that . . . ?

Conferences

For when you're talking at a conference or event. A standard 'talk'.

Recipe

SET-UP (10–15 PER CENT OF YOUR TIME):

1. Set the tone.
2. Create curiosity.
3. Answer their biggest silent questions.

MIDDLE:

Three to five chunks.

END:

- Summarise.
- Recommend the next action.

Guidance

Put yourself in the seat of your listeners: they (probably) know the topic of your talk.

If you were them, what would you be hoping for? Here are three possibilities:

1. The speaker will be: interesting, engaging, appropriate? Largely, that means friendly, knowledgeable and looking like they've got their act together.
2. You're going to gain significant benefit from the talk.
3. You're going to have answers to things you're worried about.

So your job as the speaker, at the beginning of your talk, is to:

1. set the tone
2. create curiosity
3. answer their biggest silent questions.

SET THE TONE

You set the tone in a couple of ways. By being conversational and using your own words, and not being weird (especially weirdly formal or weirdly high energy), you set the mood. You help people to relax somewhat, especially if they are expecting something very formal.

You also set the tone by setting boundaries, using the kind of phrasing we discussed above: 'In this talk, I'm not going to be able to . . .', 'What I will be able to do is . . .'.

As mentioned previously, setting the boundaries for the talk allows people to relax, knowing they're in the right place, or to realise early on that they're not. It also stops every speaker's nightmare of getting questions at an inappropriate level: sniffy experts asking questions that are beyond your ability, or embarrassing beginner's questions when everyone else is more advanced (we talk about this more in Chapter 11).

Boundaries also create realistic expectations. Let's face it – you're not going to save the world in a 45-minute talk. If you've been upfront about that, you've disabused people of any impossible expectations right from the beginning.

CREATE CURIOSITY

Curiosity is the mechanism of (a) creating questions in people's minds that they want to know the answers to, and (b) not giving them the answers straight away.

The way you do this in a talk is to tell them how they will be better at solving problems after your talk.

For example, one method of doing this is to say:

'By the end of this talk, you'll have the answer to these three questions . . .'

How do you pick the right questions? Return to your planning work, and ask yourself:

> What is important to these people?
>
> In their job, as related to your topic, what do they need and value?
>
> What do they urgently want?
>
> What might they pay for, if they knew it was going to work?

How can you realistically help them within your allotted time? Tell them.

By saying they'll have the answer to specific questions or be able to solve specific problems, they're able to track where they are in the progress of the talk. See the Signposting section (page 29) for more about how this works.

ANSWER THEIR BIGGEST SILENT QUESTIONS
Thinking about these people, what silent questions (concerns, worries, preconceptions) will they have about:

- you?
- your kind of person (whatever that might mean – profession, age, gender, nationality)?
- your topic?
- anything else that could be blazing away in their mind so that they can't listen properly to what you're saying?

You can answer overtly, or by your manner, as described in Silent questions (page 33).

The overt approach is easier to mess up by misjudging what they're thinking. Demonstrating things with your manner is less risky, but some things will need words, so see how you go.

In summary: The three things to do with the first 15% of your time:

1a. Don't be weird.
1b. Set the parameters.
2.   Create curiosity.
3.   Answer their biggest silent questions.

HOW TO STRUCTURE THE MIDDLE OF YOUR PRESENTATION
Being focused on actions helps to provide a natural structure for your talk. If you're helping them solve three minor problems, or answering three major questions, then the layout of your talk becomes obvious. (I'm saying three because as it turns out, it's a nice number for a conference-type presentation, but you can go to five – more than that can be a little superficial. Someone referenced a talk at a conference I attended a while back on the seventeen pillars of innovation . . .)

CHOOSE THREE THINGS TO TALK ABOUT
Here are some suggestions:

- The three best . . .

- The three worst . . .

- The three mistakes . . .

- The three myths . . .

- The three lessons I learned when . . .

- The three things I wish I knew when I started . . .

Just make sure that these three things solve problems that your specific listeners identify as problems, or give them more of what they identify as important (you can see how helpful doing all that thinking about your listeners was now).

TIME YOUR CHUNKS
You decide what chunks you have by first dividing up the amount of time that you have available. For example, if you have a 45-minute time slot, I would recommend you save around 10 minutes at least for questions (don't worry – I'll give you my 'never-fail question-getting technique' in the 'Listen' chapter), which leaves 35 minutes.

Approximately the first five minutes of your presentation is for the introduction, or what I think of as the set-up, preparing the way for people to be able to listen. Then there is perhaps two minutes at the end for a summary. So **35 – 7 = 28.**

In this scenario, if you had five points, you'd have five or so minutes per point.

STRUCTURE EACH POINT
Here's a rule of thumb:

1. Introduce your point by signposting:
   - where they are in the presentation
   - what the benefits are of listening to this point
   - what the point is.

2. Your point needs evidence. This could be:
   - an experience of yours (highly recommended – see Chapter 10)
   - surprising statistics
   - analogies or metaphors
   - practical illustrations.

3. You'll also need to answer any new silent questions that occur to people as you come to each recommendation. What 'Yes, but . . .' type questions might they have, given what you've just said?

4. Summarise the point, signpost where they are at in the presentation and what's coming next.

5. Repeat for each point.

ENDING YOUR PRESENTATION
The end of your presentation is when you move your listeners' attention to the action(s) you would like them to take:

- Do you want them to read, write or try something?

- Do you want them to contact you?

- Do you want them to ask some questions? (I would encourage you to leave plenty of time for a Q&A session.)

If you want them to read something, what and where is it, and how are they going to remember what and where it is?

If you want them to try something, be really specific about it. Choose something that will prove immediately beneficial to them.

If you want them to contact you, they'll need your contact details, a compelling reason to contact you, and a feeling that you'll be pleasant and useful when they do.

If you want them to ask questions, there are a bunch of reasons why people either don't ask questions or don't ask good questions (for more on this see Chapter 11).

Remember: your job is not to entertain. Your job is to be relevant and helpful. Think: 'What can I do to help these people most efficiently?' or 'How can I support them in changing their life for the better, given their circumstances?'. You'll be much more inspirational this way than you will be by trying any technique to fake being 'inspirational'.

Full recipe

SET-UP (10–15 PER CENT OF YOUR TIME):

Priorities:

1. Set the tone.
2. Create curiosity.
3. Deal with major silent questions.

Options:

- 'By the end of this session, you'll have the answers to these three/five questions . . .'
- Give a story from your life.
- Match their experience by describing their current situation and where they'd like to be.
- 'I bet you're thinking . . .'

MIDDLE:

Three to five chunks (rules/questions/myths/steps/pitfalls)

For each point:

1. Signpost, including the benefits of listening to this point.
2. Evidence, then recommendation, *or*

    Recommendation, then evidence.

Evidence might include a story, with or without statistics, scenarios or reasons.

    3. Summarise and signpost.

Repeat for each point – vary the format.

END:

- Summarise.
- Recommend the next action: do, write, read, go or say?

CONFERENCE TALK TO OTHER SPECIALISTS

For when you're talking to people who share your professional area of expertise.

Recipe

For this, see the conference recipe (page 44) but include the following three aspects.

Briefing other people who share your specialism has its own particular challenges. There are three major elements to consider:

1. boundaries
2. transparency
3. jargon.

Guidance

Setting boundaries

Setting clear boundaries is even more important for you when briefing other specialists. It helps to attract the right people to your session, and to quieten your thoughts that you're not qualified to be talking on this topic.

Specify who the session is for and the information level

Focus on your answers to Planning Question 2: 'What do I want these people to be able and motivated to do after my presentation?' Ask yourself:

Who is this session for?

What knowledge might they be coming into the session with?

What level of detail do I therefore need to include?

Attract the right people to the session

If you can make it clear in your title and blurb who the session is for and what level the information will be presented at, you'll avoid a lot of the difficulties of speaking on a topic of which others have some knowledge. Don't call it an introduction session when it's actually in-depth – and if it's in-depth implementation advice on an industry change specifically aimed at people in a particular job role, make that clear in your talk title and description and in the first two minutes of your talk.

Analyse if you're qualified to deliver the session

Sometimes we think we need to be the world's expert on the topic to be able to open our mouths at all, especially if it's to other specialists. It's only if you're promising something that you can't deliver that you'll get disappointed people. If you're really clear about your outcomes, you only need to consider whether you're able to help people inside that scope.

Be transparent

There are two major areas where you need to be transparent:

- your knowledge
- your thought process.

Your knowledge: if there are limits to your knowledge on this topic (and there will be!), be clear about what you know and don't know. It's much better for your reputation – and the well-being of your listeners – if you're clear about this from the beginning, rather than misleading people and being unable to answer their questions.

Your thought process: you will have made decisions about the level at which to pitch your information and the sequence in which to present it. If you can make clear how mixed the group is (people might not realise) and what you've done to accommodate that, your listeners will be much more patient.

USING JARGON
There is a blanket rule in some parts that you must never use jargon. When talking to other specialists, they will find it strange if you *don't* use any technical terms that are commonplace in the industry. If you want to do this in the most inclusive way, the pattern is:

Technical term → Brief rephrasing in common terms

If it's a term you suspect that some people will be familiar with and some will not, then this pattern will keep everyone with you without patronising anyone. If it's a new-ish term, then feel free to actually define and explain it.

Refer to the Conference section for the full recipe (page 50).

For when you are talking on your specialist topic to non-specialists.

Recipe

For this see the Conference recipe (page 45), but include the elements below.

When talking to non-specialists, you need to get over 'the problem of knowledge': to remember what it's like not to know what you know now. Too often I see technical people thinking that they are making things simple, when in fact they are still confusing their non-specialist listeners.

It's important to think about their lack of knowledge and get over the idea of 'dumbing down' or patronising people. We can make things simple (and need to make things simple) without talking to people like they are children: it's all in our attitude.

Take the Conference recipe and add or adapt using the principles below.

Guidance

BRIDGE WHAT THEY DO KNOW TO WHAT THEY DON'T
Your main job in talking to non-specialists is helping them bring the knowledge they have in other areas to bear on your topic.

To help bridge the gap, can you provide:

- analogies
- images
- stories?

SLOW DOWN THE THOUGHT PROCESS
If you're making connections, slow down when explaining how one part moves to the next. Remember: it's not just words but new concepts you're helping people to create in their minds. This takes time.

Take time to show the relevance of each point you're making. Start the point with a clear statement of why it's important. Then explain the point with stories, analogies and so on. Then make the relevance clear again, before doing the same with the next one.

THINK BACKWARDS FROM ACTIONS
You also need to think about implementation. If they are going to take a particular action, how will they remember what to do? What can they do if they get stuck? It's your job to turn abstract concepts into an action they can take in their everyday lives.

ANSWER THEIR SILENT QUESTIONS
Sometimes non-specialists have a certain amount of fear or resistance attached to your topic. If you think they might be scared, really go into Planning Question 3: 'What can you guess about their past and present?' Think in-depth about how they might feel towards implementing your recommendations: remember that you want them to be able and motivated to take the actions you're recommending, so you need to deal with any obstacles. Then, make sure you deal with those questions and concerns during your presentation.

EXPLAIN TECHNICAL TERMS
First, decide what technical terms these people actually need to know. Then there are two options to clarify them:

1. Term, then explanation
   Use the term (say it very slowly) → Explain it using ordinary words → Give some examples

or:

2. Explanation first, then term
Explain it using ordinary words → Give some examples → Label the term (say it very slowly).

Project update

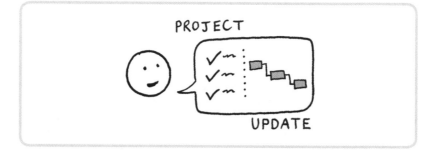

For when you're telling people about what's happened recently in your project.

Recipe

SET-UP:

- Briefly signpost what's coming up.

MIDDLE:

- Three to five areas of the project.
- Past → Current → Next steps.

END:

- Areas of change.
- Next steps.

Guidance

The project update is the workaday presentation, letting the team know what's happening. This is where a lot of the 'inspirational' advice out there falls down. Doing the project update is not a

TED talk, it's not recorded for posterity and you don't need to be entertaining. It's functional.

SET-UP
You don't need much of a lead-in. Let your listeners know what areas you'll be covering (in keywords) and what they'll know by the end.

Two or three sentences is fine, unless things are particularly complicated or it's a new group.

Be careful to not go into a history of the project: stay relevant to what they need to know.

MIDDLE
Past → Current = meaning.

The update is a chance to do just that: update.

Show progression: how things were last time, how have they changed up until now, and what this means for your listeners.

Offer evidence: stories, statistics or examples of what has changed, and the implications for them. Next, explain your plans for next steps and your reasoning.

END
Summarise again the areas of change and next steps.

If you have any requests for action, this might be where you make them, along with why they are relevant for your listeners and why you are recommending them.

IS AN UPDATE THE PLACE FOR RECOMMENDATIONS?
It might seem like all my advice about recommendations will go out of the window here, but it's important that you remain action-focused when you do an update. The actions required might be obvious, or they might be slightly hidden.

Obvious actions: these will be self-evident. If you need more resource or more time, then the actions you want to take will be either to approve your request, or at least to continue discussing it. (It will be worth your while reading the above section, 'Senior pitch', page 41, to see if any of that applies here.)

Hidden actions: there are two major sorts of hidden actions – extending the timeline, and 'non-action'.

1. Extend the timeline

For example, perhaps you don't want them to approve any more resource *this* month, but you suspect you're going to need some more for this project later. In this case, your eye is on the medium-term outcome of having that resource approved a few months down the line:

> What can you do now to reduce the impact of the silent questions they will have about your request, when you get around to making it? Can you show them that you are using current resources really efficiently? That you're solving problems well? That you're doing things in a way that means they will be happy to trust you with similar projects later?

> Perhaps you're looking to move to a new job or get in on another project? What qualities will they be looking for from you that qualify you for that, and can you hint at or demonstrate them outright with your current situation?

2. Non-action

Here, for example, perhaps you want the senior team to leave you alone.

> I was chatting with a woman who works on some really interesting community projects, setting up user-led projects on housing estates that only have a pub, shop, doctor's surgery and old community centre building. It's not very easy to quantify what the monetary benefits are, but they certainly have a huge benefit to the local population's morale. When she had to give an update to the budgetholders, she was worried that they would want to do something like send more people to observe, when what she actually needed was for the whole thing to be left alone for another few months.

If you want people to leave your project alone, that becomes the action you want them to take. So go through the planning questions.

If you were to go straight up to them and say, 'Leave this project alone for three months', knowing their past and present, what silent questions do you think they might have? Things such as:

Is the project safe?

Are things progressing?

Do I need to intervene?

Do we need to keep funding this project?

You want to present the project in such a way that it emphasises the answers to those questions and fits with what is important to them, without giving them cause to intervene:

- Show quiet competency.
- Talk calmly about problems and how they're being solved.
- Smoothly describe how the budget is being spent efficiently.
- Emphasise longer timelines than just this week or month.

Focus on the fact that you're in the middle of several things, but those things are running well.

The project update is a chance to demonstrate your skills in running a project: although it is not as overt as a pitch, it is an opportunity to begin to build your credibility for the future.

Full recipe

SET-UP:

- Give a quick description of the areas you'll cover.
- Say what they'll know by the end of your talk.

MIDDLE:

Three to five areas of the project. For each area:

- Past → Current = meaning for them (including evidence – stories, statistics, examples) → Next steps.

END:

- Summarise each area and action requests, if applicable.

Bad news

For when there is bad news you might have to give. There are two kinds:

1. **Apology**: times when you have not lived up to a standard and need to apologise.
2. **Decision**: times when a decision has been made that negatively affects the people you're talking to.

Each requires a slightly different recipe, but has a lot in common.

Recipe (apology)

SET-UP:

- Brief description of process.

MIDDLE:

- Clearly state what happened.
- Say sorry.
- List the impact.
- List probable causes.
- Next steps.

END:

- Summarise next steps (optional).

Guidance

SET-UP
You can't hang around with bad news. Keep people as safe as they can be by setting very clear expectations as to the process that is about to happen.

MIDDLE
State what happened: state it clearly and without beating around the bush.

Say sorry: a genuine apology is vital, even if you don't *feel* like it was your fault. You're part of a system that created this result, and if it has created negative impact, someone needs to express regret – and today that person is you.

Sometimes you've messed up and you clearly see it's your fault. You've made a mistake and you have to own up to it. Other times, perhaps it is an unexpected consequence of good intentions; or from your perspective, someone else's fault. The thing is, you must think this through from your listeners' perspective. If you have messed up from their perspective, you've messed up. Apologise and take responsibility for making changes.

List or describe the probable impact: it's important to show that you have an appreciation for the impact that this is having. Again, it's not the time to be running away from things.

List or describe the probable causes: this has to centre on your contribution to the problem. You can refer to other contributing factors, but be aware that this can sound like you're making excuses.

List or describe the proposed next steps: keep these provisional, but it can be reassuring to know that you've got an idea of how to mitigate the effects on the 'customer', and to reduce the chances that it will happen again (if that's relevant to the group you're addressing).

Be ready with each of these sections, but also be ready for it to break into discussion at any time. Do your best to cover all of these sections by the end of the conversation.

END
This is optional: summarise the next steps. If there has been a gap between when you started talking about the next steps and now,

then summarise them again, especially if the discussion has added to or changed them.

Full recipe

SET-UP:

- 'I have some bad news for you. What I'd like to do is tell you what happened, what the impact is as I see it, what I've identified as some of the causes, and what action I'm proposing to take.'

MIDDLE:

- Clearly state what happened.
- Say sorry.
- List or describe the probable impact.
- List or describe the probable causes.
- List or describe the proposed next steps to mitigate or prevent future reoccurrence.

END:

- Summarise the next steps (optional).

Recipe (decision)

SET-UP:

- Briefly describe the process you're about to follow.

MIDDLE:

- Bad news.
- Causes.
- Next steps.

END:

- Summarise the next steps (optional).

Guidance

SET-UP
Again here, it's a good idea not to hang around – it's best just to get on with it.

MIDDLE
Clearly state the bad news: avoid beating around the bush; use unambiguous, everyday words.

Clearly state the causes: tell them why this has come about, in broad terms.

Clearly state the next steps: people will want to know about the future, particularly what happens after the meeting and in the following days and weeks.

END
Summarise the next steps: if there has been a lot of conversation between discussion of the next steps and the end of your presentation, reiterate what's going to happen next.

ABOUT GIVING BAD NEWS
If the problem is well known, then you don't have much choice but to deal with it straight away. It's the elephant in the room. However, do remember to remain focused on outcomes – what do you want these people to be able and motivated to do:

- Do you want them to let you keep the project going?
- Do you want them to extend the timeline, or release more budget?
- Do you want them not to fire you?

You have to think about what you know about the specific people you're talking to, what you know about their past and present, and what's important to them.

As a rule of thumb, when someone has made a mistake, people appreciate a calm acceptance of mistakes made, a simple apology, then the specific actions that are being taken to reduce the impact of the event and minimise the chances that it will happen again.

Expect emotion from the people you're talking to, and be ready to breathe and listen (it can help to practise the calming techniques discussed in Chapter 7).

Your manner in these situations can do wonders. You will need to expect forceful questioning, so the more you can stay unclenched and keep breathing slowly, agree where you can agree and avoid the phrase 'Yes, but . . .', the more professional you will come across.

If you really are worried for your job, you may have to do some deeper digging related to your anxiety (for more detailed advice, head to Chapter 7).

If the bad news really is news to the people you're addressing, you're going to have to be ready for their likely reactions. People can react erratically to surprises: adrenaline takes over heads (and bodies), and reactions can be exaggerated. If you are surprised by their surprise, you'll have exaggerated reactions too, and things can turn quickly into crazy drama.

Full recipe

SET-UP:

- 'I have some bad news to tell you. I'm going to tell you what it is, why it's happened and then what's going to happen next.'

MIDDLE:

- Clearly state the bad news.
- Clearly state the causes.
- Clearly state the next steps.

END:

- Summarise the next steps (optional).

Awareness-raising

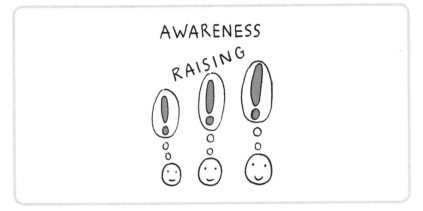

For when you're informing people about something new.

Recipe

SET-UP:

- Life without your solution.
- Life after your solution.

MIDDLE:

- How it solves their problems.

END:

- Invite them to do something.

Guidance

FOCUS ON ACTION
This recipe is for you if:

- you need to let people know about something new, but perhaps you don't have an objective say in how much they participate in it

- you're heading up a new project and you're doing a roadshow
- you've got a new business and are doing a talk to let people know about it
- there is a new initiative, process, procedure or change.

Planning Question 2 is about the actions you want the people in the group to take. Getting an awareness-raising session focused on actions can be slightly challenging, but going in with the idea that you want people to 'know about' your service, product or idea is kind of crazy. How are you going to filter what you're going to say – you've got a *lot* to say, right? How do you prioritise this?

The default position would be to give them a 'high-level' view; but without actions, how will you know if you've been successful? Moreover, without the emphasis that an action-focused presentation provides, all of your points seem to carry the same weight. That similarity equals blandness.

So, think about what you'd like people to do as a result of your talk. Do you want them to go somewhere (either virtual or physical)? What do you want them to do when they get there?

I saw a great example of this a few weeks ago. The founder of a local online community gave a 10-minute session at a local technology meet-up to present his website project. Instead of presenting a bland history of it, or 'showing people around', he decided to have an outcome that was: 'people sign up'. So he described the site, the benefits and the kind of people that it would appeal to, then he got everyone to stand up. You could sit down if you were already a member. If not, he got you to get your smartphone out, navigate to the site and sign up on the spot. When you'd done so, you could sit down.

Now, you might not want to go quite so far as publicly shaming people into taking the action you're recommending, but having an action focus helped him to get his outcome; and yes, he got a lot of sign-ups that night – including me!

INTERNAL PROJECT

If you're heading up an internal project:

- Do you want people to head to your project site and bookmark it?

- Do you want them to email you in the future when they have a particular problem?

- Do you want them to tell people they know about your project? If so, which specific people in what specific situation, do you want them to inform – and how would you like them to inform them?

NEW BUSINESS

If you've got a new business, obviously a medium-term outcome is that people buy your products or give you cash in some way. However, in the short-term, what would be a good step in that direction:

- Do you want them to get their (virtual or physical) hands on your stuff and give you feedback? If so, what specific kind of feedback do you want, and by what means?

- Do you want them to contact you if they are in a specific situation in the future?

NEW INITIATIVE

If you're rolling out a new initiative:

- Do you want people talking about it? If so, who do you want them talking about it to, and in what way? As in, using what words?

- Do you want them to display a poster, put out a card or mention it on social media?

Clear obstacles to action and link to benefits

The more you can focus on the actions that you want people to take, and the more you focus on Planning Questions 3 and 4, the clearer it will become as to what needs to be included in your presentation.

If you can get down to the nitty-gritty and really think about what might get in the way of them taking those actions, you'll see straight away that they need some specific information (as well as needing to feel and think certain things).

For example, if you want people to contact you, they'll need your email address and some clear triggers in order to remember to contact you.

If you want your listeners to refer you to others, they'll also need to trust that their reputation is going to be looked after.

CREATING REFERRALS

Referring someone is a tricky transaction, as people don't want to be thought of as weird by the people they are referring you to. If you only have a small amount of time, or your service is pricey, unusual or feels risky in some way, your outcome might need to be to do with the people in the room. Your aim becomes that *they* have more interaction with you to build trust, so that *then* they will refer you to other people.

Answering the silent questions they have about referring will include being non-weird in your manner, showing yourself not to be pushy, and nice; also competent and experienced enough so that they know you can follow through on your promises.

CLEAR THE NITTY-GRITTY OBSTACLES
When you are doing an awareness-raising session, a focus on curiosity, on people wanting to know more, is key. How can you pique their curiosity and encourage them to want to know more?

If you have a service that people might not regularly need, but will know they need it when they need it, provide them with your contact details so they have them at the moment it comes up.

Most of what you're doing in an awareness-raising presentation is making your service or project relevant: that might mean glossing over some of the aspects that don't apply to your listeners.

1. DESCRIBE LIFE WITHOUT YOUR SOLUTION
Stories work well for this. You can tell the story of when *you* realised this was a problem, or give an example of how it was a problem for someone else. You could even tell half of the story and pause when you describe the size of the problem, at the 'all is lost, I've tried everything' moment (for in-depth advice for how to find stories and tell them well, see Chapter 10).

If your service doesn't solve a problem that applies to the people in the room directly, make vivid what the problem is for others. Appeal to your listeners' desire to be helpful.

2. DESCRIBE LIFE AFTER YOUR SOLUTION

Did you describe one or two problems in your introduction? Then, describe life after your solution, when the problems you have set up in the introduction are solved. Stories can be good here too: what moment can you describe that shows the real benefit of the solution? Make sure you link to Planning Question 4 a lot: connect to what's important to the people you're addressing.

3. STRUCTURE VIA BIG CHUNKS

Lay out the big chunks of what your project or service does, how it actually solves the problems you describe. Make sure you're answering the silent questions that these specific people will have, as opposed to questions other people might have or the questions you wish they had.

Use contrast here to demonstrate clear 'before-and-after' pictures: use stories or examples, case studies, testimonials, statistics – whatever you've got.

4. GIVE THEM SOMETHING TO DO

How much of a case have you built? If you have built a very relevant and urgent case for these people to help themselves, you can ask them to do something significant. If you have built curiosity but little more, the action you request will need to be smaller, otherwise it won't register.

Summarise again the benefits to these people of taking the actions you recommend – and have a good Q&A (for guidance on how to get questions and answer them confidently, see Chapter 11).

Full recipe

SET-UP:

- Life without your solution.
  - What is the problem?
  - For whom is it a problem?
  - How big is the problem?

MIDDLE:

- Life after your solution.
  - How will life improve after your solution?
  - Give three to five ways that your solution actually solves the problem.
  - Give clear before-and-after contrast.

END:

- Ask them to take a specific action.

1 hr 50

✔	STEP 1:	GET TRACTION	30 MINS
✔	STEP 2:	REFINE ANSWERS	20 MINS
✔	STEP 3:	CHOOSE RECIPE	60 MINS
NEXT	STEP 4:	NOTES & TIMINGS	45 MINS
	STEP 5:	PLAN SLIDES	15 MINS
	STEP 6:	REALITY CHECK	10 MINS

4.
Plan your notes and verify timings (45 minutes): Step 4

Why you should use notes

I'm going to recommend something that sounds a little old-fashioned, but bear with me. One of the concerns that people have about doing a talk is what to do if their mind goes blank. Forgetting what you want to say is one of the reasons that PowerPoint (and its cousins) are used so much. The slides serve a triple purpose of handouts, speaker notes and visual aids, when they should only really serve one (for more in-depth advice on what to do with them, see Chapter 5.)

If people use PowerPoint as notes, their rhythm is controlled by the software. It becomes 'new slide, new point – new slide, new point'. This makes for a bland presentation, and also has the potential for disaster if the slides go wrong, as they often do. The more technology is involved in something, the more moving parts, the more chance there is of something going awry.

The process I'm going to describe will help you to:

- be flexible and adaptable to what's happening on the day, in your situation
- easily remember what you want to say
- keep to your allotted time
- prepare a presentation in only as many minutes as it needs.

However, without complex slides, how are you going to remember what you're going to say?

How to produce usable notes and test timings (45 minutes)

1. Get a piece of paper.
2. Write your big headings, the big chunks, as keywords, with some space in-between.

3. If it's, say, a 45-minute session, subtract a couple of minutes for the introduction and at least 10 minutes for Q&A, maybe 15 minutes.

4. Divide the remaining time between your (three to five) headings.

5. Set your timer. Talk about one of those headings. When you feel like you've done it justice, check the time. Were you under or over?

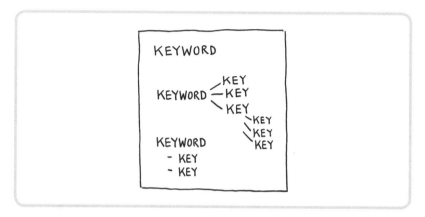

If you were over – and almost certainly you were – focus again on your outcome. What are the actions you want people to take as a result of this bit of your presentation, and your presentation as a whole? Focus a bit tighter on that, then go again.

If you were under, is there some extra evidence you could give? Are you setting up your points with benefits? Are you signposting? Are you answering silent questions? Are you summarising? Don't add material just to fill time, but if it's really feeling sparse, make sure you're using all the ingredients well.

Practise once or twice until you're virtually hitting your target for that section. Then go on to the next section. Allow this to be the first draft and very loose.

Refine

1. Go back to your notes. If you keep forgetting something, add in some more keywords under each heading as reminders. What do you want to make sure you include?

2. Once you've got all the sections reasonably down, add some numbers beside each point. If the beginning of the talk is zero,

write the number that the timer will be at when you hit the start of each point. Alternatively, you could do a countdown.

```
2·00    KEYWORD

6·00    KEYWORD
        -KEY
        -KEY    KEY
12·00   KEYWORD KEY

18·00   KEYWORD
        KEY
        KEY

24·00   KEYWORD
```

3. Run through the whole thing once or twice, using your notes as a prompt in front of you (but not in your hands). Get a sense of the flow of your talk, and have enough keywords so you can deliver it reasonably well.

 WARNING!
Do not video yourself – it's not going to build your confidence at this stage.

Now you have your notes so you can deliver your session.

What if you are woefully over time?

If you are feeling like you have to cram stuff in and talk super-fast, you need to lower your expectations of your outcome:

What would be a more realistic outcome?

Can you go from complete project sign-off to agreeing to speak more?

Can you go from people agreeing to volunteer weekly hours to your project to having them sign up to the mailing list?

Can you go from changing their practice so they are faultless with the new legislation, to knowing when they need more information and where to get it?

It may be disappointing to lower your expectations, but it's much better to realise this now than just before, during or after the event. Almost always we try to bite off more than we can chew when we're planning a presentation.

> **! WARNING!**
>
> You might be feeling a temptation to go back to old ways, to give a briefing or lecture on the big chunks of knowledge. Hang in there. You've worked too hard to move away from your new, action-focused approach. You want to stay engaging and interesting, right? You want to do a presentation that builds both your reputation and the reputation of your project. Doing a theory-based lecture will not do that, but keeping relevant and action-focused will.

Myths about presentation notes

Myth: You have to memorise your presentation

There is a weird myth floating around that you need to memorise your presentation, to know it by heart. This comes from a 'performance' mindset, where the speaker becomes a performer, so therefore needs to remember their 'lines'.

Radical as it may seem, I recommend that you use notes when you are presenting. It's not a performance. If used as I'm about to describe, notes are totally professional and actually increase your impact as a speaker rather than reduce it. No one cares if you remember your talk – they care about relevance and utility, and how the information you're giving them helps make their life better.

Myth: Looking at notes is unprofessional

One mistake I see people making when they start using notes is to talk about the fact that they're using them. They apologise if they have to refer to them: 'Sorry – I'm going to have to look at my notes!' – as if looking at notes is some kind of failure.

The rule is: if you talk to people, look at them.

The reverse of that is true: if you're not looking at people, you stop talking. So, if you're looking at your notes, you stop talking. If you're looking at a slide, you stop talking. If you're looking at the flipchart, you stop talking.

Looking at notes is a silent activity. When you've looked at your notes and you're ready, look up at your listeners and resume speaking.

Myth: Silence is bad

Think about when you need to refer to notes. It's almost always when you're moving from one section of your presentation to the next. If you look at your notes in silence, then all your group experiences is a pause. As listeners, we need pauses, so your pause becomes a place where your listeners can naturally digest what you've just said and get ready for the next part. It's much better to look at your notes and stay on track than it is to waffle, go off on a tangent or dry up (for more about why it's important to learn to pause, see Chapter 8).

Myth: A script is better than notes

I was running a workshop a few weeks ago and following my part were two representatives from a company which provides software that allows you to take the details of visitors to a stand at a trade expo. They were two bright young women, one of whom did the talk and the other who acted as technical support afterwards, when people were trying out the software. The company had obviously made a decision to go with slides and a script – and it was professional in a way, I suppose.

I do get why organisations make that decision. They get a consistent standard of delivery, but unfortunately that 'standard' is almost always a synonym for 'mediocre'. It makes me sad when I see a talk such as this, because with just a good set of notes and bit of practice (probably less practice than she'd spent reading the script out), the rep would be able to talk fluently about her product in a much more engaging way, and deal with questions without making the questioner feel like they were interrupting her flow.

Myth: You'll forget what you're going to say

In order for you to be able to work from notes, they need to be sufficiently thorough that you know you're unlikely to miss out something essential. Aim for keywords and phrases that are organised, so that you can see the logic of your talk easily.

Start with keywords with a bit of space between them. Then add in subpoints underneath, or to the right. Phrases are fine too (if there are technicalities you need to remember word-for-word), but not sentences. Once we start writing sentences, we start to lose our faith that we can form ordinary, conversational sentences like we do all day.

Think about a meeting you've had recently. It could be with a group of people or just a one-on-one chat. Maybe you did a bit of thinking beforehand about what you wanted to discuss, but did you write a word-for-word script? That would be ridiculous, right? Thinking we need to write a script is only because somewhere we've lost faith that we can speak naturally in front of a group. With sufficient keywords, you can.

When you might need a script

The only times you might need to speak from a script are if you are giving a legal statement to the press and have to be careful about being quoted, or if you are the president of a country, who has to phrase things very carefully because it will be picked over. If you're not in one of those situations, keyword notes will be fine.

Where to put your notes

You have a few choices as to where you put your notes.

On a sheet of paper

This is the one I tend to go for: I put the paper near me, written or printed out in large enough letters that I can read it without having to lean over it. Paper allows me to write in last-minute reminders and has no technology that might go wrong.

Index cards can work too, but don't hold them in your hand if you can help it.

On a huge sheet of paper

If you are at a big conference or you're in a situation where you don't have a table nearby, I would recommend you put your notes on an A3 or A2 pad. Get a big marker pen and transfer your notes onto the pad. Once you get to the venue, work out how to have the pad in your eyeline. If it's a small enough room and there aren't lights in your eyes, you can put it up at the back of the room. If you're on a stage, it easily could be flat on the floor, where you can glance down at it. Get to the venue early enough that you can work this out with whoever is managing the space.

On your PowerPoint notes

You could put your notes on the Notes section of your PowerPoint slides. This makes me anxious for you for a couple of reasons.

First, technology goes wrong – *a lot*. A technical error could render everything useless.

Secondly, you need to be able to see the notes. This will mean that you either need to be close enough to your device to see them, or the technology needs to be set up so that your notes are visible on a screen that you can see.

Again, liaise with the event manager or whoever is running the technology – and be sure to have a back-up on paper, whatever you do.

2hr 35

✔ STEP 1: GET TRACTION   30 MINS
✔ STEP 2: REFINE ANSWERS 20 MINS
✔ STEP 3: CHOOSE RECIPE   60 MINS
✔ STEP 4: NOTES & TIMINGS 45 MINS
NEXT STEP 5: PLAN SLIDES 15 MINS
     STEP 6: REALITY CHECK 10 MINS

5.
Plan visual aids that support your outcomes (15 minutes): Step 5

After preparing with notes, your next step is to consider visual aids.

Do you really need slides?

Slides often serve three purposes: speaker notes, handouts and visual aids.

Speaker notes: you've got notes to remember what you're going to say, so no slides needed here.

Handouts: if you'd like people to have a takeaway after the talk, create a handout separately from any slides you're going to use during your talk. You can either make a physical document or, if you're sharing your slides online, a set with enough detail to stand alone without you there to talk about them.

Visual aids: your one and only question is – 'Do these people need a visual aid to progress towards the action(s) I would like them to take?'

If so, make a slide; if not, then don't. When would they need a slide? Well, the Lightheart Slide Rule is:

If they'd need it in conversation, they need it in a presentation.

Imagine you're talking one-on-one with one of your listeners. Would you need to get out a pad and pen and start drawing a diagram? If so, then they may need a visual aid in a presentation.

If you do need slides (15 minutes)

If you do find that you need slides, here's my best advice.

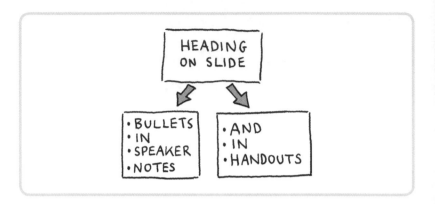

First, practise your presentation so you can talk by just using your notes. This way, the slides won't dictate the rhythm of your talk. Then:

1. Take your big three to five headings.

2. Make a slide for each, just putting the keyword for that section in the middle of the slide. No bullet points! Bullet points lead to boring and bored-sounding 'I'm reading a list' voice intonation, which is terrible to listen to. Just put the heading in the centre of the slide in big type.

3. Put the bullet points into your notes.

4. Put the bullet points and maybe a bit of clarifying explanation into a handout.

5. Make the handout available before your talk if you're happy for people to be looking at it as you speak, or afterwards either online or on paper. If you want people to contact you, make sure your handout has your contact details on it.

Yes, you could design some fancy slides with 'funny' or beautiful photos, but think carefully whether your listeners really need them, and whether you have more effective uses for your time. If you've thought deeply about relevance and usefulness, and are making recommendations tailored to the group in front of you, you won't need gimmicky slides to be 'entertaining' or 'inspirational'.

Useful, relevant and conversational is going to take you much further than aiming to be 'entertaining'.

If your topic is complex

If you need a visual aid to make a complex concept visual, here's a crash course in doing just that.

- Grab a piece of paper.
- Draw three lines across the page and three lines down the page to split it into 16 boxes.
- Draw:
  - (a) A, B and C diverge
  - (b) A, B and C converge
  - (c) A leads to B leads to C
  - (d) A leads to B leads to C leads to D, which cycles back to A
  - (e) A overlaps with B
  - (f) A overlaps with B, B overlaps with C, C does not overlap with A
  - (g) A, B, C and D are at different levels
  - (h) A changes into B
  - (i) A is loosely connected with B
  - (j) A is contained in B, which is contained by C
  - (k) A is more important than B, C is least important
  - (l) A is growing more important, B is growing less important

  Making connections: using just symbols, you can show that A and B are more connected to each other than they are to C, D and E by:
  - (m) Making them nearer to each other (proximity).
  - (n) Making them the same shape as each other (shape).
  - (o) Making them the same colour as each other (colour).
  - (p) Making them face the same direction as each other (direction).

Below is an example; yours will be different. The idea is to see that you can make concepts visual with only a little thought.

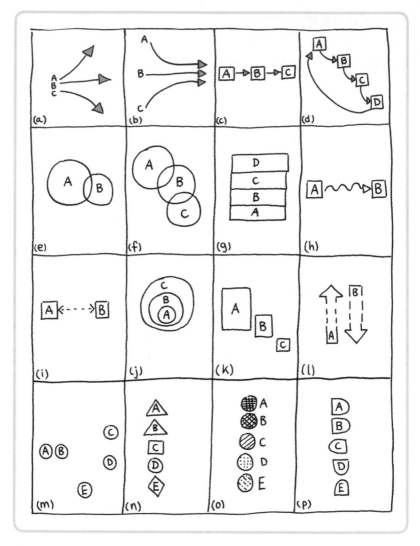

Think: what is the relationship I'm wanting to clarify? How can I make that visual?

If you have a concept that builds up

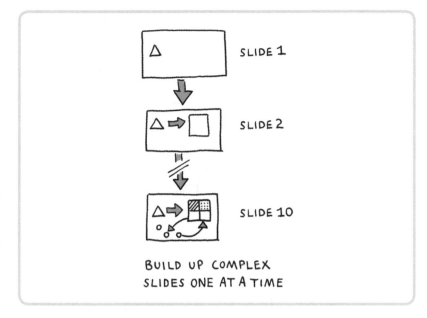

Start with a simple foundation visual.

Copy that slide, and add the next logical step. Repeat.

Make sure each slide only adds one more progression, so the picture gradually builds up for your listeners.

You can do this also with a complex bit of text. Not so hard, eh? Just takes a shift in mindset.

> **TIP**
>
> If you find you're spending an enormous amount of time learning to use the actual PowerPoint design tools, search online for templates or draw it out by hand, take a photograph and use that as your slide.

Special situations that need more slides

There are three situations that might require more slides than normal.

1. **You live in a strong PowerPoint culture.** If the people you're hoping to influence expect PowerPoint, you may well have to produce some slides or they may think you're unprepared. A way around this is to let them know that they'll receive a thorough handout. In this way, they will know you've prepared well, and can relax and listen. (When people request the slides in advance, they want to find out what you're going to cover. Sending them the slides and the handout serves the same purpose.)

2. **Conference calls** (see Chapter 12: Conference Calls, page 149).

3. **Cross-cultural situations** (see Chapter 13: Global Communication Strategies, page 161).

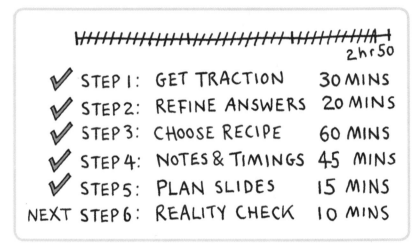

6.
Lower your nerves with a reality check (10 minutes): Step 6

You've spent almost three hours and quite a bit of energy so far in putting together a presentation that seems able to do the job.

Now it's important to check that your presentation is likely to be on target. Sometimes we get caught up in an initial idea, but we need a reality check to make sure that all the pieces are the right ones, and in the right place. We also need to check that we're not fooling ourselves about likely outcomes.

Outcomes

The first place to return to when doing your reality check is the outcomes (Planning Question 2): what actions do you want people to be able and motivated to do during and after your presentation? Having looked in detail at:

- what might be going on in their heads – their thoughts and feelings
- their current situation
- practical hurdles such as time and money
- emotional ones such as motivation

– are these outcomes likely and probable? Are you being realistic in expecting people to take these actions, just from listening to your presentation?

Don't be surprised if you have to downgrade your expectations at this point. If you were expecting a whole big chunk of action, do you need to downgrade it to the first couple of steps in that direction? Remember, often you're just starting a conversation, not putting a full stop on the whole matter.

Able

Are people able to take the actions you want them to take? Remember the resources they might be missing:

- time
- knowledge
- skills
- budget
- people
- technology
- equipment.

How much of this are you able to address in your presentation? If you need your listeners to take action to get something they are lacking, then you need to treat that as an outcome for your presentation.

For example, if they need to go and get some knowledge (look something up, read something) in order to be able to do the prime action that you want them to take, it's your job to get them to be able and motivated to do that beforehand.

If they'll need budget or equipment, you'll need to point them in the direction of getting it (including thinking through the barriers that they might have in connection with this, and why it's important to them that they do so).

Are your recommendations realistic and probable, bearing in mind what they might be missing in order to be able to take that action?

Motivated

People are *able* to do plenty of things, but they don't *want* to do all of them. Have you made the benefits of your recommendations clear to the people in front of you? Unless you make it very clear how following your recommendations is going to help them get more of what they want, they are unlikely to take action.

Silent questions

What do you know about their past and present? What silent questions will those experiences bring? Have you answered those silent questions implicitly with your manner, and explicitly with words? Are you feeling nervous because there are questions you're dreading that you aren't ready to answer? (For more on this, see Chapter 11 on answering overt questions, page 131.)

Timing and level

As you practise your presentation out loud, are you rushing to fit everything in? Are you giving the level of detail that your listeners need in order to move in the direction of your recommendation? Do you need to simplify more? Alternatively, have you hit the limits of your knowledge? Do you need to change the boundaries of the session by altering the title or setting expectations towards the beginning?

Is your presentation appropriate to the time of day that it's happening? Have you ended up with more points than were originally in the recipe? Are your slides simple and easy to digest?

> **TIP**
>
> **Recommendation about your title and talk description**
>
> As previously mentioned, be careful that when you get to writing your talk title and blurb, you make it clear who it's pitched at and at what level the information will be (we'll return to the importance of this in Chapter 11).

Style

Is this a presentation you can actually deliver? Does it fit your style, or is it too much of a stretch? Setting yourself a bit of a challenge is okay, but overhauling your personality is not.

If any of the above areas need tweaking, then go ahead and tweak them.

How to know you're ready

Don't wait to *feel* ready: we rarely feel like we've prepared enough. Here's your checklist for knowing you're ready:

1. A set of keyword notes sufficient for you to remember what you want to cover and no more, with fairly accurate timings next to

each point so that you know where you need to be, and by when. These notes remind you to make the benefits clear and answer silent questions as they come up.

2. The simplest slides you can get away with – with no full sentences, and avoiding bullet points if at all possible (optional).

3. Some sort of takeaway – a handout and/or more detailed slides that your listeners can use as a reference for your content afterwards (optional).

Things you do not need to know to be ready to deliver your presentation:

- You do not need to feel a Zen-like sense of calm.
- You do not need to know your presentation by heart.
- You do not need a script.
- You do not need a whizzy set of beautiful slides.
- You do not need to put on a mask, or pretend to be different to what you are.

Ask yourself: do I have what I would need in order to have an organised conversation with one or two of my listeners about this topic?

That's what you need to do a presentation. Got that? You're ready!

HHHHHHHHHHHHHHHHHHHHHHHHHHHHHHHHHHHHHHH

✓ STEP 1: GET TRACTION   30 MINS
✓ STEP 2: REFINE ANSWERS   20 MINS
✓ STEP 3: CHOOSE RECIPE   60 MINS
✓ STEP 4: NOTES & TIMINGS   45 MINS
✓ STEP 5: PLAN SLIDES   15 MINS
✓ STEP 6: REALITY CHECK   10 MINS

PART 2
SPEAK

Now you have the content for your presentation in some sort of order, you can turn your attention to the ways you can improve it.

Five key speaking skills

We'll be focusing on five areas that give you immediate benefits.

Calm

If nerves are a major concern for you, this chapter will give you techniques and strategies for lowering adrenaline, so you can reduce your dread of presenting and think clearly.

Steady

This chapter deals with the non-verbal aspects of speaking to a group that help you come across as credible and confident.

Natural

If you can speak fluently in conversation, you can speak fluently in a presentation. This chapter will help you develop a conversational style of speaking, so you will sound natural and engaging to your listeners.

Story

One of the major ingredients of speaking in a way that captures people's attention is the ability to talk about things that have happened to you in a captivating way. Stories work as compelling evidence for your recommendations, and this chapter will give you what you need to know about how to use stories in a presentation.

Listen

A presentation is usually only one part of your interaction with a group. Action almost always happens after you've had some sort of conversation. This chapter makes sure your presentation leads to good questions and that you are ready to answer them confidently.

Quick wins, next steps and take it further

Each of the five chapters has a similar layout.

Quick win

Each chapter begins with a 'quick win'. This is an exercise or experiment you can complete in under 20 minutes that will immediately increase your skills.

Next steps

If you'd like to increase your capability in an area, then you can follow these steps. These guide you through practising your abilities further.

Take it further (online)

This book is focused on immediate improvement. If you have the time and inclination to really build your skills, these online chapters go deeper into more analysis of presentations, causes and remedies for problems and in-depth change. The 'Take It Further' chapters are at **andrewlightheart.com/presentationnow**

If you'd like to improve on all fronts, move through the quick wins for each section. If you'd like to go further into one particular area, follow the quick wins – next steps – take it further sequence for that topic.

7.
Calm

Why it's important to be calm

Adrenaline and anxiety are the cause of many symptoms of bad presentations. Adrenaline is the hormone that makes your heart beat faster, your mouth go dry, your palms sweat, your stomach drop and your feet go cold. It has one major job: to limit your ability to make slow, rational decisions and to prepare your body to survive imminent physical danger. It also limits your ability to remember anything that is outside of survival.

In terms of presentations, when speakers get nervous they lose access to many of their higher-thinking functions. This leads to fast speech, less flexibility to respond to surprises and an over-reliance on slides and notes.

If you lower your adrenaline you'll be more resilient, more able to respond to unexpected questions and more credible. You'll also stop dreading public speaking quite so much!

There are many causes of anxiety, and the following section gives strategies that approach how to be calm from several different angles. Learning to be calm is a meta-skill in that it increases your ability to use all your other speaking skills. It is a skill well worth investing your time in.

Quick win

Anxiety may come from several sources, so we have to work with it from several different angles.

The most direct route is through the body. My advice is to implement a simple technique right now, and practise it as much as you can. In the literature on overcoming anxiety, one of the phrases that sticks is that strategies need to be well-practised, so they are streamlined and ready when needed. Basically, because anxiety and adrenaline interfere with your ability to think calmly, you need not to be making decisions about how to deal with the anxiety when it's happening. You need to press 'Go' on the strategies you've already prepared. This is an apparently simple strategy, but it's deeply effective if practised.

The importance of unclenching

Imagine a horror movie. The protagonist is near the monster, hiding in a dark place. Are they breathing fast or slow? Fast, right? Are their muscles tense or relaxed? Tense. That's how the body behaves when it's under threat. It's making sure, among other things, that enough blood gets to the muscles, ready to move at a moment's notice.

That is fine for situations of physical danger, but the system that evolved to survive predators is over-triggered by our modern environment. Our body moves into this response far too often, which turns into what we identify as anxiety and stress.

When you're talking to a group, you want to feel safe. A good way of making that happen is for your body to mimic what it does when it's safe, by breathing slowly and relaxing your muscles.

EXERCISE: PRACTISE UNCLENCHING (10 MINUTES)

1. Take a moment to slow down your breathing. Breathe in for a count of four, pause for one, then out for four. Wait until your in-breath happens spontaneously (this helps you not to hyperventilate!) and repeat. Whenever you feel anxiety, your first remedy is your breath.

2. Increase the impact of your breathing by relaxing your muscles. Take a couple of minutes to sit in a chair and

➔

---

relax your muscles from head to toe. Relax the muscles in the top of your head, your forehead and your eyebrows. Relax the muscles around your eyes, cheeks, jaw, even let your tongue spread out on the bottom of your mouth.

3. Keep breathing slowly as you relax your neck (maybe move your head gently from side to side), roll the tension out of your shoulders, relax your upper arms, lower arms and your wrists and fingers.

4. Take a deep breath in and breathe out slowly as you relax your chest, stomach muscles, upper legs, lower legs, ankles and toes. (Sometimes it helps to clench a muscle before you relax it – it releases tension easier that way.)

5. After you've been all the way through your muscles, if you have time, take a second tour, noticing particularly the muscles around your eyes, jaw, neck and shoulders, which is where tension is often held.

The more you practise, the more the benefits will be available when you need them.

I would recommend:

a. At least one 'full' practice every day: 5 minutes. Schedule a reminder for this to come up somewhere: first thing, last thing, after lunch – whenever works best for you.

b. A 'mini' version 10 times a day (yes, 10 at least!). The mini-version is: relax the muscles around your eyes, jaw and neck, slow your breathing and look around you.

I sometimes get anxious in everyday life, and this one practice has changed things for me massively. Whenever I feel my body go into defence mode, I know how to slow down and encourage safety.

It's a gradual build-up, this quick win. It's more like water softening some hard earth, rather than some 'kapow!' magic trick.

Follow these instructions, and you'll feel the benefit when it comes time to stand up and do your talk.

Next step 1: Go Wide

As well as retraining your body, there's a bit of mental jiggery-pokery which helps lower your nerves. It's important to realise when the source of your nerves is the horror movies you're making in your mind.

HOW I STOPPED BEING SCARED OF HEIGHTS

One of the things that I've had to learn to be okay with is heights. I get very scared up in high places. I love to go up high, getting a view over the landscape of a city, but if I'm not careful I go into full-on survival terror. (Ask me one day about when I went up the Sagrada Familia cathedral in Barcelona and walked down the stone spiral staircase sobbing – not pretty!)

What I've realised is there are certain situations in which almost everyone is scared, and other situations in which only a few people are scared. In an earthquake, I would imagine pretty much everyone is scared; but, for example, in a glass-bottomed cable car, or at the top of the Eiffel Tower, I appear to be in a minority of people who are scared.

This tells me that it can't be the situation that is making me scared. It must be something I'm doing in my mind.

Horror movies, directed by you

The mind makes little distinction between what is vividly imagined and what is really happening. This is why you can watch a movie and feel real happiness, real sadness, real fear. When you turn your attention to a situation which isn't inherently dangerous but in which you feel scared, you'll find that you're running a horror movie in your mind.

When I'm up in high places, I realise that I run a horror movie of me falling. I look out over the edge and part of my mind imagines the ground coming up towards me, again and again. Unsurprisingly, this sends my body into survival terror. In addition to learning to physically unclench (as in the quick win), I find that noticing what is really happening in that moment helps me to reduce my adrenaline.

→

'Am I actually falling right now?' No. I feel my feet on the floor and the floor is steady.

'What can I see?' I can see walls, the floor, some trees below.

The same principles apply when you start feeling scared about presenting.

Getting conscious of your thoughts

When it comes out of the blue, anxious adrenaline often comes from something you've just thought. Really examine the thoughts about your presentation that cause you anxiety. As you practise unclenching, you become really sensitive to when your nerves are rising and pay attention to what has triggered them:

- Did you just think about all those people looking at you?
- Did you just think about *that person* asking you *that question*?
- Did you imagine yourself fumbling with the slides?
- Did you just imagine your mind going blank?
- Did you just check how ready you feel, and found it was not at all?
- Did you just imagine you could hear the thoughts of your listeners, and how bored they are and how much they hate you?
- Or something else?

Getting to feel calm is not hard work. You can make a great deal of progress if you learn how to place your attention on what is actually happening right now.

I do this by doing what I call 'Go Wide'.

EXERCISE: GO WIDE (5 MINUTES)

1. Place your index fingers a couple of feet in front of your face. Keep looking straight ahead, then move them sideways, right hand to the right, left hand to the left, until they disappear from view. Then bring them back in until you can just see them in your periphery. Wiggle the fingers if that helps.

→

That's your peripheral vision. Widening your peripheral vision helps you to stop being so focused on what's going on in your head.

2. Ask yourself: what do I see?
Notice what's in your field of vision, both in front of you and to the sides. Move your head a bit, looking at what's around you, while keeping a bit of your attention on the periphery. As your gaze falls on things, you could name them: books, painting, trees, sculpture, feet, jumper, bowl. Come into the moment.

3. You could also ask: what do I hear?
Notice the sounds inside the room and outside the room, close to you and far away.

4. If it helps, you can even notice your feet and hands. If you're sitting, notice the feel of the chair under your legs, your back.
Keep a bit of your attention on your peripheral vision, and if your body wants to take a deep breath in, let it but don't force anything.
If the sounds help you to come into the moment, listen to them. If not, don't.
If the feeling of your feet, hands and legs helps you come back to the present, then notice them. If not, then don't.

5. Then tell yourself: everything else is a thought or a feeling.

This is key. Our mind gets lost in its own creations sometimes and we don't notice. Sometimes the flash of the horror movie is really fast, so fast we didn't even realise we were thinking it – but the anxiety it provokes feels real.

By widening your peripheral vision, noticing what you're seeing and hearing, you can bring yourself back into the present moment and remind yourself that a thought is just a thought – it's not really happening.

A: Add this on to your unclenching practice: once a day, really go slow and go wide.

B: Whenever you feel anxiety climbing, go wide. It only takes a second or two, but you're retraining your mind to stay out of horror movies and in the reality of what's really happening.

Next step 2: Find Five

Fear comes from a part of you thinking that something bad is going to happen. Anxiety often comes from being overly certain of that 'bad' outcome. 'Find Five' is a technique I use when I've got a situation coming up which is causing me anxiety.

EXERCISE: FIND FIVE (10 MINUTES)

In order to counteract anxiety, try finding five possible outcomes to the situation, for example:

1. A terrible outcome, e.g. losing your job or business and all credibility.

2. A mildly bad outcome, e.g. you forget a bit of what you were going to say and maybe you fluff some answers to questions.

3. A mildly positive outcome, e.g. you get through all your points, the reaction is positive, the energy in the room is good.

4. A wildly positive outcome, e.g. you are on fire. New things occur to you that you follow, you make people laugh at the right points, and as a result you get a promotion or a new client.

5. A surprising, life-changing (and positive) outcome. (This is a bit difficult to predict because it's a surprise.) For example, what I tend to think is that I'll look back on this talk as a turning point in my life. Maybe I'll meet someone who becomes a great friend, or I'll learn something that changes my thinking on a topic, or someone will recommend a book that I love, or one of the people attending my session changes the direction of my future somehow.

→

All of the outcomes have to be possible, but not necessarily probable.

Look at each one of these five outcomes in turn, and see that they are all possible – and that actually you have no idea what the outcome of your presentation will be.

This can be reassuring, as it helps to undermine any false certainty that disaster is coming.

Next step 3: you are not going to die!

There is a part of us that thinks that giving this talk is actually going to kill us: that somehow everything is leading up to this presentation, and then that's it. If you look into the future beyond the talk, there is just the grey fog of nothingness. Unsurprisingly, this creates distress.

EXERCISE: EXTEND THE TIMELINE (5 MINUTES)

One of the best things you can do in this situation is to imagine what you're going to do straight after the talk.

Ask yourself: where will you be, what will you do? Then what will you do later that day? That evening? What is happening the next day? What will you be thinking about, who will you be talking to, what will you be doing? What do you have planned for the day after that? The next week? Next month?

What are you going to do with friends or family? Reassure the scared part of you that your life will continue. Populate your future with full-colour plans.

It's going to be okay – you will survive this.

Take It Further

For more in-depth help with presentation anxiety, head to the Take It Further chapters at:

Andrewlightheart.com/presentationnow

8.
Steady

Why it's important to be steady

There's something impressive about a steady speaker. Being able to use your voice and body to convey credibility allows your listeners to relax and feel that they are in safe hands.

This chapter helps with everything you'll need to exude confidence. You'll learn:

- How to increase your impact by speaking slowly.

- The body posture that adds gravitas.

- What to do with your hands.

- How to pause, so people remember you as a clear communicator.

Focus on these areas of non-verbal behaviour and you'll come across as much more authoritative.

Quick win

Slow down

The best thing you can do for your presentation style is to slow down. Working with speakers from all over the world for over a decade, in all types of industries, in all careers and at all levels of seniority, there is one thing I have never said: speak faster.

Three reasons why people speak fast

Nerves make us speak fast for three reasons:

1. One is that everything physical wants to move faster when we are nervous. Therefore, of course, your mouth wants to run away with itself.

2. Nerves come from our survival instinct. We want to fight and we can't. We want to run and we can't. So we want to make the discomfort end as soon as possible. How do we do that? We try to speed through our presentation as fast as possible, so we speak quickly.

3. There is psychological malarkey that goes on too: we make it up in our head that everyone is bored by our presentation. We try to speed through it so that we bore them for the least amount of time possible.

Four problems with speaking fast

There are big problems caused by speaking fast: some for you, and some for your listeners.

IT MAKES YOU DIFFICULT TO UNDERSTAND

Speaking fast makes your topic difficult to understand. Remember that this is the first time your listeners will have heard you say these words in this way, and so they need time to digest what you're saying. Even if you've made sure that your topic is relevant and you've put in great ingredients, if you're not understandable, it all falls apart.

IT BORES PEOPLE

Rather than saving people from boredom, speaking fast actually bores them more. If they can't understand your topic because you're speaking too quickly, they'll soon drift off and start thinking about other things.

IT SOUNDS LOW STATUS
Take a moment and think about two archetypes. Think about a queen. She sits in the middle, allowing others come to her. She is steady. She speaks slowly. Then think about the servant. The servant moves around, has fast movements, speaks quickly.

You don't want to trigger 'servant' in people's head. So build your credibility by speaking slowly. A slow pace signals gravitas, experience and stability.

IT SOUNDS NERVOUS
Even if you're not nervous, a fast pace makes you sound nervous. People will assume you are nervous by the fact that you're speaking rapidly.

The advantages of speaking slowly are as follows:

- You have more time to think.

- You come across as credible, experienced and senior.

- You are more persuasive, as people have more time to think about and digest what you're saying.

- You are remembered as a clear communicator.

It is a misconception that a slow pace bores people. Low energy can be boring, but slow pace is clear. Slow pace with raised energy is a magic combination. If you pitch your energy at about 5–10 per cent above your group while saying your words clearly, your charisma shoots up.

Another slightly unexpected benefit of focusing on slow pace is the beneficial effect on your nerves. By slowing down your pace, you'll find everything else slows down too, even your heartbeat.

How to slow down

When I'm coaching people and I record them speaking slower and slower, they're always amazed. What felt 'normal' sounds too fast, and what feels really slow actually sounds natural and easy to listen to. The experience of speaking slowly is a strange one, especially if you're working on this on your own.

Don't focus on slow, focus on clear.

The key to learning how to slow down is not to focus on slowing down, but to focus on saying each word clearly. Saying. Each. Word. Clearly. With. Separation. Between. Them.

The rule of thumb is: speak so slowly that you can hear each word you're saying, as you're saying it.

Have you ever tried to use voice recognition software? You know how. You. Have. To. Speak. Each. Word. Clearly? Go for that. Here's your quick win exercise.

EXERCISE: SPEAK SLOWER (15 MINUTES)

Take the notes from your presentation, stand up somewhere you can talk out aloud, take a section you feel familiar with and just start talking. Consciously say each word very clearly, with separation between them.

See if you can say each word ridiculously clearly, as if you're practising your pronunciation. If you feel like you're speaking too slowly, way too slowly, that's good. Slow down even more when saying numbers and the names of people, projects and products. We get very used to saying them fast and it can really trip your listeners up if they don't catch a name or a number (see also page 156).

Now, this is a new skill: you'll be interrupting old habits. It means that this may well feel clunky as you're doing it, not 'the way you do things' – but of all the ways you can improve your delivery, slowing down and saying your words clearly is the thing that will improve your reputation the most. Slowing down unlocks your ability to think as you're talking, and lets you deal with surprises during your presentation.

Speaking slowly does not mean speaking fast paced with lots of pauses.

Tony Blair, the former British prime minister, was known for speaking in fast phrases with pauses in-between. This is *not* the same as speaking slowly – it is clunky and strange. Do not follow his example!

Concentrate on hearing the words you're saying as you're saying them, and you'll be fine. It isn't that pauses aren't good – they are. In fact, they are essential to your listeners being able to digest what you're saying; but pauses work together with slow pace in order for you to come across as natural and not (sorry, Tony) weird.

Next step 1: body language

Your next step with becoming steadier as a speaker is to focus on the way you hold your body.

EXERCISE: BALANCED WEIGHT (5 MINUTES)

1. Imagine you have one set of bathroom scales under one foot, and another set under the other. If you were to lean to the right, the number on the right-hand scale would go up and the left one would go down. If you were to lean to the other side, the reverse would happen. Stand with your weight so evenly balanced that the numbers on the two scales would be the same. Don't lock your knees, keep them a little soft and keep your weight evenly balanced.

2. Take a concept from your presentation and talk about it out loud, keeping your weight balanced. If you want to put energy in, allow your energy to be in your upper body, keeping your lower body still.

Why this is important

In the English idiom, someone who is unsteady is unreliable, who 'blows in the wind' and can't be trusted. Someone who is steady and firm has gravitas and is reliable.

If your adrenaline is high, there is a temptation to move back and forth. A lot of the time a speaker isn't aware that they're doing this, but it can be distracting for listeners. It certainly doesn't signal credibility. Think of the archetype we discussed earlier: the queen who stays in the centre and takes her time, while lower-level flunkies are the ones who chase around. You want to trigger 'senior archetypes' in people's minds.

This doesn't mean that you never move. You need to know how to stand still, and will spend around 90 per cent of your presentation in this centred posture. If you do move, do it with purpose – perhaps to emphasise a point or to reinforce a change in content.

> **TIP**
>
> **Should I walk around?**
>
> Sometimes speakers walk around the stage. Sometimes my clients are impressed by these speakers and want to emulate them. Two things: first, often these people aren't consciously choosing to move around; it's adrenaline or nerves that cause it. Secondly, moving around can make it difficult to keep concepts clear in people's minds, as they are distracted by having to follow the speaker around the space.
>
> This doesn't mean that you can't raise your energy. I would recommend that you keep your weight evenly balanced and channel your energy into your hands and face.

What to do with your hands

Often I get asked: 'What do I do with my hands?' Well, the answer's simple:

1. Stand with your weight evenly balanced, as you practised above.
2. Bend your arms at your elbows, bringing your hands up to just below waist height.
3. Then forget about your hands.

Your hands know how to gesture along with the rhythm of what you're saying. I have come across perhaps one speaker in my whole coaching career who had to tone down his gestures. Everyone else has been totally fine; when they bring their hands up and forget about them, their gestures support and reinforce what they say.

KEEP YOUR HANDS APART
However, something that does need to be avoided is linking your hands together. You see people clasping their hands, crossing

their arms or fiddling with their wedding ring. Body language books say that these things 'mean' something. That when you have your arms crossed, you're closed to ideas. That when you have your hands crossed behind you, you are hiding something. I'm not a body language expert, but I doubt that is what these gestures 'mean'. It could be that a person who crosses their arms is defensive, but also it could be that they are cold or they just do that habitually. Or maybe they're self-conscious about their outfit, or they've just noticed a stain and they're hiding it. No one can really know.

If as the speaker you cross your arms, you are communicating *something* – and that something will be different depending on the people who are watching. It's not a neutral body posture.

If you notice yourself linking your hands together across your body in some way, drop your hands so that they hang loosely by your side. In this way you won't communicate something you don't want to communicate.

Having your hands by your side feels weird at first, but looks good. The only way of making it feel less weird is to practise.

EXERCISE: NATURAL HAND GESTURES (5–10 MINUTES)

1. Take a section of your presentation. Stand with your weight evenly balanced and start talking.

2. Bend your arms slightly at the elbow, then let your hands do what they want to do. You can experiment a bit by really letting them be very expressive, just to calibrate what that feels like.

3. If you find your hands linking with each other in some way (clasping or playing with a ring, for example) let them drop by your side.

4. When they want to gesture again, let them.

5. Keep going for 5–10 minutes.

Your focus is on keeping your hands separate as you talk.

WARNING!

Please don't plan your gestures: a steeple here, a firm cutting gesture there. It's simply ridiculous and looks that way. Also, it means your attention is on you, not on the people listening. Just let your hands do their thing.

TIP

Allow this to be strange at first. You're bringing consciousness to something that has been an unconscious process until now, so it is going to feel a bit clunky. Stable body posture and uncrossed hands are two things that seriously increase your credibility when you're speaking, and so are well worth working on.

Next step 2: pauses

Speakers sometimes treat their listeners like they're fractious toddlers who need constant entertaining, otherwise they're going to lose focus. While this is not always totally untrue, it can be translated into action in an unhelpful manner: speakers don't pause.

Pauses are highly desirable and feel about 10 times as long for the speaker as they do for listeners. When I run a presentation skills masterclass, I always get people to listen for when each speaker pauses, and what it does for them. Here's what people have told us about pauses over the years.

Pauses are important for listeners

THEY GIVE PEOPLE TIME TO DIGEST

A long stream of words hitting people with no let-up is like feeding someone one mouthful after another without giving them time to chew. When you pause, people unconsciously take time to process what you've told them, and are able to relax and follow what you're saying.

THEY HELP LISTENERS TO CHUNK INFORMATION

When you pause between thoughts, your listeners get a little space, a little paragraph break between that thought and the next. This means that they are able to track the structure of what you're saying easily, and will remember you as a clear communicator.

THEY EMPHASISE YOUR KEY POINTS
When you pause before and/or after a keyword or key point, it makes it stand out, as if it's been highlighted in people's minds.

Pauses are important for speakers

THEY LET YOU THINK
When you pause, it's most often between one point and the next. By pausing, you give yourself time to gather your thoughts before moving on.

THEY GIVE YOU TIME TO CHECK YOUR NOTES
Keeping on track and not losing your thread is really important. Pausing between points lets you have a glance at your notes. Remember: all the listeners experience when this happens is a pause – and they like pauses.

THEY HELP YOU RESET YOUR PACE
If you ever find yourself speeding up and losing control of your 'runaway train' mouth, pauses help. Pause, take a breath, reset your pace and continue speaking. You get back in the driver's seat, as it were, and slow things down.

EXERCISE: PRACTISE PAUSING (15 MINUTES)

1. Take your notes for your presentation. Notice the sections and subsections.

2. Start practising out loud.

3. As you get to the end of a thought, allow it to sink in. In my mind, I think: 'Send . . . [wait] . . . received. Send . . . [wait] . . . received.'

4. Keep going for 15 minutes.

Don't aim straight for pauses, and certainly don't start thinking about writing pauses into your sentences. The way you're going to make this natural is to become conscious of the sections and subsections of your talk, of the transition from one idea to the next.

Err on the side of exaggeration. It's much better to provide very clear and distinct thoughts, rather than have your content all roll into one undistinguished onslaught. Notice how much pausing helps you feel more in control.

Take It Further

Go deeper into being a steady speaker in the Take It Further chapters at:

Andrewlightheart.com/presentationnow

9.
Natural

Why it's important to be natural

In this chapter we'll be working on your speaking style. Style is a difficult issue. We admire other people's style and naturally we want to emulate them. I recommend that you borrow from other people's structure (the sequence in which they put their information, or how they use signposting, story and so on), but never borrow their style. Copying someone else's style is hard work, too often comes off as fake and is totally unnecessary! Using your natural style means that you attract people to your own style of working. If you pretend to be someone else, you'll have to maintain that mask for the rest of the relationship.

Your style needs to be all yours. You, and the way you speak normally, are enough. If you can have a conversation about your topic, you can do a presentation.

The skill is moving your conversational skills into the context of doing a presentation.

That's what we're going to focus on in this chapter.

Quick win

We do ourselves a disservice by the very way that we think about presenting. A lot of nerves and heartache come from wanting to be entertaining, to give a performance.

The performance metaphor

The roots of the performance metaphor are understandable. Most people have experienced a performance, and doing a presentation has many apparent similarities. People are sitting looking in the same direction, maybe even in theatre-style rows. In addition, there is a person at the front whose role it is to keep the attention of listeners.

NEGATIVE IMPLICATIONS OF THE PERFORMANCE METAPHOR

Performers 'rehearse' a sequence of material prescribed in advance. They have a word-for-word script. They are expected to be entertaining, inspiring or to provide a moving, hilarious or beautiful experience for the audience.

Audiences are mainly passive consumers of an offering, with responsibility for the success of the performance lying solely with the performer.

Using this as a metaphor leads to a stressful experience for a presenter.

Actors often end up teaching presentation skills, as they have spent years learning to perform in front of a group. They often talk about adrenaline and nerves being required for them to do a good job, and how they would be worried if they felt calm. If you've read through Chapter 7: Calm, you'll see how ridiculous this is in terms of the type of presentations you need to make.

The bottom line is: actors pretend to be someone else and say someone else's words.

I want you to go exactly in the opposite direction.

I want you to be more yourself and use your own words.

We need to change the metaphor that you use when you think about presenting.

Conversation works better as a metaphor

What does conversation imply?

- More than one participant (and I mean participant, not passive audience member).

- A certain amount of planning or agenda, but certainly no script.
- An ordinary style – 'conversational' – with a level of formality that fits the relationship between participants.
- People just being themselves, not wearing a mask.
- An appropriate level of detail and jargon.
- Generally less stress – contrast 'giving a performance' with 'having a conversation'.
- Probably not trying to change the world – 'just' a conversation.
- Little room for planned gimmicks, jokes or slogans.

Yes, doing a presentation is a slightly strange type of conversation, but as a metaphor it can take the heat off you a lot. The conversation metaphor allows you to connect genuinely with the people in front of you and get your message across.

DOES BEING CONVERSATIONAL MEAN BEING INFORMAL?

I was running a workshop for Women Who Code, an organisation designed to inspire women in tech careers. Someone who works with senior people said that she wasn't sure that 'just having a chat' would work with them.

Of course, that is true. While a conversational style is often less formal than a written speech, it really means: 'If I were in conversation with these people, how would I talk to them? How formal or informal would my language be?'

The quick win exercise below will make things clearer.

EXERCISE: CHANGE YOUR PRESENTATION TO A CONVERSATION (10 MINUTES)

1. Go to Planning Question 1: 'What do I know about the people I'm talking to?' Look at the subgroups you identified, and imagine sitting down with a representative from two or three of the major subgroups.

→

2. Imagine discussing the topic with them, moving through your points and explaining your concepts (you can even try doing this out loud).

3. Notice at what level of detail you describe the concepts, the kind of words you use, how you explain jargon (or not), and so on.

4. If you were in conversation with them, what would you most emphasise? How would you answer (or pre-empt) their questions and concerns?

5. Look back at your presentation plan. What lessons can you apply immediately to your approach? Make your presentation as conversational as possible.

Conversational style makes being interesting easier

From your listeners' perspective, there is only ever one person listening: them. If you speak in a conversational style, people respond more in the style of a conversation partner rather than passively listening. This doesn't necessarily mean that they say things, or that they display the facial expressions and body language of someone who is having a conversation, but their listening attitude is different.

Think about how much spoken communication in your day consists of conversation. It might be overstating the case to say that we have evolved to be attuned to conversation, but it's certainly true that we are very accustomed to it. The more you can speak as you would if you were in a conversation, the easier it is for people to tune in to your topic and track your ideas.

From your perspective, speaking conversationally is a style much easier to maintain than an unnatural one-way speech. Planning a presentation, and not trying to be someone you aren't, makes the process much less work.

Next step 1: how to make your voice sound good

I do work on helping people improve the sound of their voice, but I don't do a lot with people on technical voice work because:

- Relaxing your jaw, neck and shoulders immediately produces a warmer voice.

- Slowing down means that you say your words more clearly.

- Most people don't have the time, money or need to work intensively on the techniques of speaking.

- People concentrate too much on how they are speaking, rather than on the way their words are being received.

- Focusing on your intention to communicate does a lot of the work for you.

Intention to communicate

I worked with a singing coach once, and she said that you have two ways to approach the mechanics of singing. The first way is to learn the anatomy of the way that voice is produced and gain conscious control of your diaphragm, sinuses, vocal cords and so on, to produce the sound you'd like to make. The downside of that is, even after a lot of study, figuring out how to use all those physical aspects at will is extremely hard. We aren't built to do that.

The second way is to remember that when you are singing, you have an intention to communicate something. Even from the way you breathe in, you're thinking of what you want to say. She would get me to say 'Hey! Hey!' like I was getting someone's attention then, when I was singing, to keep that focus on the words of the song. **Remember your intention to communicate with your listeners**.

The same is true of doing a presentation. The more you can remember your intention to communicate, the more engaging your style will be.

EXERCISE: IMPROVE YOUR VOICE BY FOCUSING ON OUTCOMES (15 MINUTES)

1. Make your style even more engaging and conversational by going back to the outcomes that you established in Planning Question 2.
   What actions do you want these people to take?
   What do you recommend?
   What do you want them to be able and motivated to do?

➜

2. List how their life will be better if they follow your recommendations. Really imagine what would happen if those people took the actions you'd like them to take. Why is this genuinely a good thing?

The more you focus on your intention – to create the circumstances for them to follow in the direction you are recommending – the more you'll be conversational. Your whole body and voice will work together to communicate with your listeners in a warm and engaged way.

WARNING!

Don't overdo it

Remember: your intention to communicate does not mean 'going hell for leather' or 'whooping it up'. Passion can be a good thing, but a facsimile of passion is ultimately empty (and weird). Really look at the people in front of you, set the space for them to take action, and speak normally to them as you would if you were in conversation.

Advice on eye contact

Speaking of looking at the people you're talking to, this is probably a good time to think about eye contact. You will recall from Chapter 5 on visual aids that a Lightheart rule is:

If you are talking to people, look at them.

WHY EYE CONTACT IS IMPORTANT
1. You are talking to people. It's polite and normal to look at them in the same way that you would if you were in a one-to-one or small group conversation.

2. Looking at individuals reminds you that you're talking to real people, not to a homogenous crowd.

3. People like to feel seen.

HOW TO MAKE EYE CONTACT

1. **Make true eye contact, not fake eye contact.** Fake eye contact means turning your head and face around the room as if you're making eye contact, but actually you're looking near people's faces. True eye contact means really looking at people and making contact. Look people in the eye, speak a few words to them, then move on to a different person.

2. Yes, this can make you feel vulnerable, but practising unclenching and going wide helps (see Chapter 7). A certain feeling of vulnerability when people are looking at you is only natural. If you're not accustomed to it, it takes some getting used to. This doesn't mean that vulnerability is bad or that you're broken, it indicates that you are human.

3. **Try and talk to everyone.** I know this is crazy in a big room, but aim to make contact with each individual. Make sure you include the people at both edges (I notice most speakers have a preference for looking at one side or the other), the people in the middle, and the people in the back corners. I've heard people recommend that you draw a pattern with your eye contact in the room. My fundamental disagreement with these methods is that they make you *look* like you're making contact with people, instead of *actually* making contact with them.

4. **Always be talking to someone.** Speak as if your message can only be heard if you're looking at someone. If you're talking to the room in general (or worse still, the PowerPoint slide), you've forgotten who is in the room. Always be making eye contact with someone – not the same someone, though. Move to a new person every few seconds.

How to help everyone feel included

Here's an interesting phenomenon that I only learned by coaching so many groups in presentations. As you're speaking, if you can linger a little longer on each person – not so long that it's creepy, but long enough that you feel contact – what people say afterwards is that it felt like you were talking just to them; but everyone feels like that.

How to make eye contact from the stage

Sometimes you might find yourself on a raised platform or stage, perhaps with lights. It can be hard to make eye contact with the people you're talking to in that case, because it's too dark.

What you do here is to think about where people are sitting. I've been known to turn up before an event starts and sit in the seats at the back, in the corners, at the front and in the middle, just to get a sense of what it's like to be sitting there. Then when you're talking, make sure you look out at all the places where your listeners are. See if you can 'feel' them listening, even if you can't see them, and look at them.

If you're ever in a theatre where people are on different levels (the circle and so forth), make sure you look up in their direction too. Your job is to make your recommendations, so have the intention to connect with the people who are actually there – wherever they're sitting.

Next step 2: find things in common

When I was putting together my first workshop on cross-cultural communication, I did a lot of research into prejudice and attitudes. What particularly interested me was how we specify who is 'us' and who is 'them'. A study came out of that reading – and I know that a lot of this brain scan stuff is oversimplifying matters, so let's use this as a metaphor for how people look at other people.

For example: when a non-homeless person is shown a picture of a homeless person, parts of the brain that correspond to 'objects' light up. Slightly terrifying, but not beyond the bounds of possibility, right? Sometimes when people seem very different to us, we treat them like objects. In the context of presentations, I hear people saying they'll be talking to 'the business' or 'some architects' or 'a bunch of n00bs' or 'the board'. We stereotype people based on one aspect of their life: their job role, for example.

There is a second step to the experiment. Show a non-homeless person a picture of a homeless person and ask: 'What do you think their favourite vegetable might be?' *Person*-related centres of the brain light up.

When we remember that the person in front of us is complex, with needs, wants, preferences and a life outside of their role, we see them as a person again.

This is super-important when you're presenting, as it's all too easy just to see a sea of faces.

Treating the people you're talking to as just their roles – just architects, just 'the senior team' – means you're going to make odd choices about what you say and how you say it. When we treat a group of people as a homogenous mass, we don't speak in natural ways.

Presenting to a group of human beings as a faceless category is bad for us in two ways:

1. We'll be making very unsubtle decisions about what to say and how to say it. 'Business people are interested in profit,' we'll decide, or 'Parents just want what's best for their children.' These statements lead to patronising, simplistic and superficial communication. This in turn produces either loads of awkward questions and objections to your recommendations or, worse, disengaged silence.

2. If you're just speaking to categories, you won't engage patterns of 'human being' communication. Patterns of intonation, gesture and language that are so natural in conversation become strained and unnatural. If what you're looking at is a small set of broad categories rather than a collection of individuals, you won't come across as a real person. In fact, you'll come across as someone who is 'presenting' with no regard for who is in front of them.

WHAT'S TRUE ABOUT HUMAN BEINGS

Your first remedy for inauthentic communication is to think in detail about what you know about who you are going to be talking to. If you want to be more authentic in your communication, you have to remember that you are a real person, and so are they. There is actually no *group* in front of you – just *individuals*.

➜

Here is what's true about them. They have difficulty balancing the demands of work with the demands of the rest of their life. Pretty much everyone is not doing what they dreamed of doing when they were nine years old; if they are, it's not how they imagined it to be.

Some of them will be parents. Most of those parents will think they're not doing a good enough job.

They are looking for purpose in their life. Their body isn't quite the shape they'd like it to be. There are things they've always meant to do which they're beginning to think they might never get around to doing. There are things they wonder about, things that disgust them and things they dream of doing.

There are particular foods that make them smile. They have hobbies, interests, passions, likes, dislikes, yearnings, loves and hates. They have a favourite vegetable.

They're messy – they're real, just like you. They're not inanimate objects or mere categories.

Good – but I can't talk about that!

Now, I'm not saying that you mention any of this overtly. This preparation is mainly for you. Partially it's so that you can choose your material and make it match who you are talking to; but mainly so that you can remember to talk to them for real, with ordinary language.

If you're doing the same presentation to a different group of people, remember that you have to go through this process for each group. Even if you come up with similar answers, it keeps you aware of the real people who are in front of you.

EXERCISE: FIND THINGS IN COMMON (20 MINUTES)

1. Take a sample person who might be listening to you talk. Get them clear in your mind – it might be a person you've actually met, or a composite sample person.

2. List 10 things that you may have in common. Make at least half of them items that are not connected to your or their job title, for example:

   Do you live in the same city?
   Did you do similar training to them?
   Do you think you might share similar preferences for mornings? Food? TV shows? Holiday locations?
   If you both live in the same country, what will you both have seen on the news recently?
   What do you think you have in common in terms of values, of what's important?

3. Now take someone else and come up with 10 things that you have in common with them. See if you can make at least five of them *different* things than you had in common with the first person.

4. Repeat this process twice.

5. Now think about standing up to recommend things to that group of people.

Do you feel the collection of real human beings that are in the room? Good. Keep a sense of that as you're talking to them.

Take It Further

Continue to develop your speaking style by going through the Take It Further chapters at:

Andrewlightheart.com/presentationnow

10.
Story

Why it's important to tell stories

You may have heard that including stories in your presentation is A Good Thing. But why?

Our mind is built for stories

An anthropologist did a meta-study on all 6,000 human cultures that have been studied. He found a bunch of things that exist in all human cultures: the concept of right and wrong, showing your status by what you wear on your body, rules about hairstyle (search the Internet for 'human universals' and there's a whole list).

One of those things is gossip and myth. There is no human culture ever studied where people didn't tell stories. It makes you think that there must be something in our minds that craves story.

Books that last for hundreds or thousands of years are, by and large, stories. Stories are the way that information is passed inside organisations. When you go and work for a new boss, what's the first thing that other people do? 'You're working for her? Well, I heard . . .' If you start a new project or work on a new product, your colleagues tell stories about their experience of it. We call it 'gossip', but it's the informal network of how information is passed.

What do we spend our lives reading, watching? Do we spend money to sit in a room and watch two hours of trees blowing in the breeze? Two hours of fish swimming in the water? No! We go and watch stories. We read novels. We watch TV series.

Our brain hungers for stories

If you can put some stories at the right level into your presentation, you'll find that it's going to make you more interesting. Stories are almost inherently interesting.

Ever keep watching a series that is actually pretty terrible? Ever finish reading an awful book or persist with a ridiculous film because you wanted to know what happened at the end? Stories engage the mind in a way that little else does, so it's vital to work on this aspect of your presentations.

First, find stories to tell!

Quick win

Find stories to tell

Something I often hear is: 'But I don't have stories to tell – my life is boring!'

Well, if you're looking for 'entertaining' stories, you're going to find it hard; but you don't need entertaining stories to move people in the direction of your recommendations. You need stories that serve as evidence. (In the next steps we'll focus on how to tell these stories in an engaging way, but also how to *choose* stories and focus on finding evidence for your points.)

Stories do a really good job of convincing. If you've ever interviewed anyone for a job, what you're looking for is stories of when they've actually done things they'll need to do in the new role. Stories give information on the way you approach something, your personality and attitude. They convey much more than bare facts.

Stories are more convincing, partly because the details you give are easy for your listeners to picture, and partly because story structure is inherently persuasive.

So, where do you find stories?

STORY-MINING

You're going to have to go back through your life, thinking of stories. A really good way is to think of problems you've solved.

EXERCISE: STORY-MINING (20 MINUTES)

1. Get a piece of paper and draw a line. One end is your birth and the other end is now. Mark on significant events – moving house and jobs seem to be significant milestones which remind you of other changes in your life.

2. Go through each of those areas and do a bit of brainstorming about problems you've encountered and solved. This is not the time to be going back over traumatic times, but just think: what issues did I face, and how did I get through to the other side?

For example, my line would show:

Moving to the United States when I was a kid – first house after school – college – information technology trainer – moving in with my husband – living and working in Asia – moving back to live with mother-in-law – moving to Birmingham.

Off the top of my head, as a kid I lived in Houston, Texas and they thought I had a speech defect – I didn't pronounce my 'r's correctly: 'fatherrrr', 'motherrr'. I was sent to speech therapy, effectively to correct my British accent.

When I was a training manager, for example, I had to train all the staff in all different types of topics to do with communication. I very quickly learned to research a subject and put together an engaging learning session using adult learning principles.

Moving to Birmingham, I had to learn to get involved in networking meetings, which (for a secret introvert like me) was properly scary.

You'll see that at each juncture, you can come up with 5, 10, 20 different challenges you faced and got through. **Don't worry about how to tell these stories yet.**

You'll learn to tell stories well in the next couple of sections of this chapter. Do the exercise above (maybe tack it to the wall and add to it over the next couple of weeks), and you'll see that story-finding is a breeze. You'll never find it difficult to find useful stories again. For now, go through your timeline, identify major milestones, list the challenges you moved through and problems that you solved (big and small), and we'll come back to it later. I promise you, you'll look back on this as a major step towards becoming the kind of speaker you want to be.

> **TIP**
>
> Think about the presentation you're planning and which points need supporting evidence. Using the above process, focus in on the job you're doing right now, and especially on the project you're going to talk about.
>
> What problems have you encountered? What didn't go well? What problems have you solved?
>
> Then you'll have some examples for your presentation.

Next step 1: choose the right type of story, at the right level

Telling stories in presentations is not hard. Follow the instructions in the following two steps and you'll have enough knowledge to do it well.

> **EXERCISE: CHOOSE THE TYPE OF STORY YOU WANT TO TELL (10 MINUTES)**
>
> The type of story you tell depends on your purpose for telling it. Here are three story types to get your thinking going.
>
> **Warning story**
> A warning story is a way of making a limit clear, of saying: 'If you go all the way over here, bad things will happen.' For example, if you're recommending that people adopt a certain standard, tell a story of a disaster that happened when you didn't follow that standard. This might be an occasion for using a story where you were not the main protagonist, but were involved

→

enough to know what was happening. Avoid urban myths: the further the story is from your experience, the less it will engage people's attention.

To be compelling, the story needs to demonstrate that not following your advice means that your listeners will lose something important to them. (This will be helped by the presentation preparation you've done: focus particularly on Planning Question 4: 'What is important to them?', which is connected to the things that your listeners need and value.)

Benefits story

This is the flipside of a warning story. Talk about a time when you followed your recommendation and things turned out really well. Make sure that the things you talk about gaining are things that your listeners value. Talking about a time when you learned a mnemonic for a coding rule might be super-appropriate to other software engineers, but for a group of landscape gardeners, maybe not so much.

Analogy story

When you're explaining something that your listeners may find strange or complex, that is when you need an analogy. Analogies give people something to grasp, something from their current experience.

Analogies start with: 'It's a bit like . . .'.

Analogy *stories* start with: 'It's a bit like when I . . .'.

To choose an analogy story, decide:

1. What aspects of this topic need to become clearer to my listeners?

2. What else are they familiar with that shares one or more of these qualities?

3. What has happened to me from that familiar domain that helps highlight that quality?

Here, don't immediately dismiss non-work examples.

EXERCISE: CHOOSE THE RIGHT LEVEL OF STORY ZOOM

I spend a lot of time working with clients on their ability to tell stories smoothly, in a way that adds to their credibility. Often people default to the wrong 'zoom level' when telling stories. Zoom level is my way of referring to the amount of detail you include in your story – are you zoomed out all the way so you're sharing very little detail or are you zoomed in very close so lots of detail is apparent? For ease, we'll refer to three levels of story zoom, each with a different level of difficulty, impact and risk:

1. snippet
2. full event
3. extended set piece.

Snippet

Zoom: looking at the story from far away

Difficulty level: easy

Impact: minor

Risk: low.

Snippets are what inexperienced storytellers default to initially when I ask them to tell stories. They are the lowest risk, but also the lowest-impact way of introducing your experience. Snippets are one-to-four-sentence examples of things that have happened to the speaker. They go something like: 'We had a client who got into trouble doing this. As soon as they started implementing our system, they soon saw things turn around.'

This is okay, but it's hardly attention-grabbing. It doesn't give your listeners much to get their teeth into.

Snippets are good for a bit of 'spice' and perhaps a bit of variety, but need not be the only form of story in your presentation.

Full event

Zoom: actual size

→

Difficulty level: medium

Impact: significant

Risk: medium.

Full events are stories about a specific event that happened on a specific day or series of days. It's about a time that you faced a specific problem and came out the other side. Normally it takes between 1 and 4 minutes to tell. Fascinating, natural speakers tell stories at the full event zoom level.

Extended set piece

Zoom: super close-up

Difficulty level: hard

Impact: potentially life-changing

Risk: very high.

Extended stories take perhaps 10 minutes or more to tell. They are highly practised and sometimes can constitute the whole of a presentation. Inspirational speakers – former sportspeople, mountaineers, etc. – often use them as the basis for their talks.

Every now and again they are beautifully done, and can provide an immediate and moving message that drives an idea home deeply. However, mostly they come off as over-rehearsed, stretching a point or just being told for the sake of it.

Almost categorically I would recommend that you avoid these stories – the risk of messing up is much too high.

Next step 2: learn to tell a story really well

The four parts of a full-event story

Mainly, I recommend that you tell full-event stories. There are four parts to telling this type of story so that it grabs people:

1. context
2. the problem

3. actions

4. the result.

It almost doesn't matter how 'interesting' or 'significant' the story seems to you. If you include these elements (and emphasise them in the way I'm going to suggest later), you'll have a story that attracts and holds people's attention.

EXERCISE: PRACTISE TELLING A STORY (10 MINUTES)

Select a story you might want to include in your presentation. Set a timer and tell it out loud including these four elements.

1. Context – start by saying when this story happened, where you were, who you were with and what you were doing.

2. The problem – the thing that makes a situation a story is the problem that you solved. Tell us about the problem. Why was it particularly important or hard for you in that moment?

3. Actions – what sequence of actions did you take?

4. The result – end with the happy (or sad) result.

Check how long your story took to tell. If it was shorter than you wanted it to be, go back and elaborate on the four story elements. If it was longer than you wanted it to be, streamline some of the detail. Follow these rules like a recipe. Make sure you have all four ingredients in that sequence, and you will be golden.

Three things to avoid when telling a story

DON'T MAKE IT UP

It's hard to tell a story that isn't yours and, what's more, your listeners will feel it. In order to engage your listeners, find a story from your life that fits the point you're trying to make, and tell that one. Why make things harder by making things up?

DON'T EMBELLISH

There is no need to add in extra drama. I've heard thousands of stories in presentations and believe me, if you have the above four ingredients in the right order, your story will be more than fine. If you want to amp it up, I've got advice for you in the next chapter, but embellishment or exaggeration are not the way to go. Plus, if people find out that you're not telling the whole truth, they can feel betrayed and think badly of you.

DON'T SABOTAGE YOURSELF

I see presenters decide that they're going to tell a story, then halfway through they begin doubting themselves. They start to comment or apologise for how 'boring' their story is, they skim over the four ingredients, or they miss things out to speed through their talk – then their story is rubbish. Don't do this. If you've started on your story, follow the four ingredients all the way through to the end.

Four mistakes of inexperienced storytellers

Avoid these four mistakes and your stories will have much more impact.

NOT ENOUGH CONTEXT

Make sure you set the story in its temporal context. As mentioned previously, tell us when, where, who, what. Who said what to whom? Don't take off before your listeners are on board. Without context, we don't feel like we're listening to a story, and so none of us get the benefit that stories bring.

NOT ENOUGH SIGNIFICANCE

Did you ever go to a movie and find the plot less than gripping? Get to the end and find it unsatisfying? Often this will be because the writer hasn't made you care enough about their characters, and/or didn't make those characters go through sufficiently hard times. Stories grip us when we really see how the main character (that'll be you) is really up against it.

I've heard great stories about insignificant events. Tiling the bathroom, getting a chest of drawers up three flights of stairs, starting a new running habit, specifying an outsourcing project. Stories do not have to be life-alteringly massive to be engaging.

We have to understand why, in that moment, this problem was hard.

We have to understand why, in that moment, this problem was important for you to solve.

Make the stakes really clear.

If you show us why this was important to you, we'll be rooting for you when you work on solving it.

SKIMPING ON DETAILS OF ACTIONS
If you have made the significance of your actions clear, we'll be interested to know what you did to solve the problem.

Don't skimp on details (while sticking to your zoom level – full-event stories are normally 1–4 minutes long).

THE RESULT IS INCONCLUSIVE
Don't wimp out on telling us how things ended up. If it's a warning story, describe the repercussions. Don't exaggerate, but describe. If it's a benefit story, let us really see the happy ending.

TIP
Storytelling is an art form at which writers work hard. For you to use stories in presentations, particularly for full-event stories, follow the advice above and your impact will rocket, just from talking about things with which you're familiar. Make the effort to include stories, and you'll notice your listeners being much more attentive and involved.

Take It Further

Learn more about telling compelling stories in the Take It Further chapters at:

Andrewlightheart.com/presentationnow

11.
Listen

Why it's important to listen

The flipside of speaking is listening. This is when you think about your group asking you questions. Before we come to strategies to deal with The Dreaded Q&A, it's important that you ask yourself a question.

Why do you want people to ask you questions?

Aren't some of your worst presentation nightmares about answering a question badly? Isn't encouraging questions just opening the floodgates to difficulty and embarrassment? Wouldn't it be easier if you just muttered, 'Any questions?', let everyone sit in silence for a few seconds, and then you just sat down?

I know you might be saying, 'Yes, it would be better.'

However, once you think about how the Q&A fits into things, it can help you refocus on the purpose of your presentation. When you think about the aims of your presentation, you soon realise that having people ask you questions leads people faster toward your outcomes – and, in a way, this is the point of doing a presentation in the first place.

Q&A and the purpose of presentations

If you've followed my advice and planned around the actions you'd like people to take, you will have realised that as soon as you think about the response you're looking for, things become much clearer.

Generally, the short- or medium-term outcome for a presentation is conversation. It's rare that a presentation leads directly to action. All being well, almost always a presentation will lead to a conversation which, in turn, will lead to action. The reason you're giving the presentation is to spark that conversation and set the frame for it – and by conversation I mean the exchange of ideas in many formats, as well as a literal 'I-say-something-you-say-something'.

If conversation is the thing, if you want people discussing your topic, surely a Q&A is exactly what you're looking for?

If your answer was 'no', let me add something else.

If you want people discussing your topic and *you knew how to deal well with difficult questions*, isn't Q&A exactly what you're looking for?

(There is some advice later on in this chapter to help you start thinking about how to deal with difficult questions.)

WHY YOU MIGHT WANT QUESTIONS AFTER A PRESENTATION
- You want to know what people don't understand, so you can correct their understanding or fill in some information that they might be missing.

- You want to know people's concerns about your topic, so you can help them deal with them.

- You want to know what's of interest to your listeners.

- You want to have been an interesting speaker.

- You can't bear the silence any longer.

If you can work out why you want interaction, you can begin to work out how to make it happen.

Quick win
How to get people asking questions

So you finish your presentation. What's next? You ask, 'Any questions?' and then silence, the howl of the wind . . . . If you want questions after your presentations (and you should), think about what might be getting in the way of people speaking out.

It's difficult to give things to practise with questions, so this quick win is how to think about and approach the Q&A session.

Eight barriers to people asking questions

Why do people not ask post-presentation questions? Here are eight reasons.

THEY'RE EMBARRASSED TO BREAK THE SILENCE

It might be the silence: they might not be confident to speak in front of a group. Just think about how nerve-wracking it is as the speaker to speak in front of the group. You had a chance to plan your session, and yet having all those eyes on you can still be hard. The same thing might be true for your listeners.

THEY DON'T HAVE ANY QUESTIONS

It might be that there aren't any questions to ask. This is likely to come from two factors:

1. What you spoke about was totally irrelevant to them (unlikely, but possible).
2. You were just too comprehensive.

If you genuinely have given them everything they need to know, there really might not be any questions left to ask.

THEY HAVEN'T HAD ENOUGH TIME TO PRODUCE A QUESTION

If you go straight into the Q&A the second that you finish your presentation, sometimes people haven't had enough time to process the information and find the gaps. I'm a front-row question asker and I notice that, as a listener, I need a few seconds to come up with what I might want to ask about. Often, speakers give up after just a few moments of silence, which might not be long enough. (Be especially careful with this in cross-cultural situations – different cultures have different tolerances for silence.)

THEY DON'T THINK THEIR QUESTION IS RELEVANT OR GOOD ENOUGH

If there is silence, people might not be sure if they have a question that's 'good enough'. They might not be sure if it's too personal, or if they might be revealing their own ignorance. Instead of embarrassing themselves, they stay silent.

THEY DON'T THINK THE SPEAKER WANTS QUESTIONS

Sometimes the speaker's attitude as they ask for questions signals that they would much prefer it if the group didn't ask them questions. They seem to just want to sit back down and have the experience over with, or they have a forbidding attitude and people daren't ask questions. People pick up on the body language and back down from volunteering a question if they think that it's not going to be received well.

THEY NEED SEEDS OR SUGGESTIONS FOR TOPICS

If you've talked about quite a broad topic, people might not be able to choose which question to ask you. This is the opposite of not having any questions to ask. It still means you don't get any questions, but it may be easier to solve.

THEY'RE CONFUSED

In theory, being confused is a reason to ask questions; but in truth, if people are unsure they may well stay silent.

THEY'VE FORGOTTEN THEIR QUESTION

Maybe they had a great question but by the time you ask them, they've forgotten. This used to happen to me as a listener a lot until I worked out how to fix it.

Now we've spent five minutes thinking about the problem, I bet you're already seeing some ways of fixing it, right? I have some ideas about strategies, so keep reading.

Practise strategies to get people asking questions

Here are some strategies to get people past these hurdles and asking post-presentation questions.

PRACTISE WHAT TO SAY AT THE START OF YOUR SESSION

First:

- Let people know in advance that there will be time for questions.
- Invite them to note down their questions.

Which might go something like this:

> There's no way I'm going to be able to cover this whole topic comprehensively in such a short time. I'm going to keep some

time at the end for questions you're still bound to have, so feel free to note down your questions as we go, so that when it's time, you've got them to hand . . .

– or however that might work in your own style.

EXERCISE: PRACTISE YOUR SET-UP (5 MINUTES)

1. Decide what you might say and practise it *out loud* three times.

2. Add a couple of keywords into your notes to remind you.

When it comes to asking for questions

- Suggest some topics.

- Include words other than 'questions'.

- Include some pre-question private time.

For example:

So, that's enough of me talking. I bet you still have some questions, some concerns, some unanswered thoughts. Maybe they're about [list some aspects of your topic]? I tell you what, turn to the person next to you, say 'Hi' if you haven't met them before, and compare notes for a minute or two about anything unresolved for you about this topic.

Nod, smile and turn away, leaving the group to follow instructions. There will be five seconds of absolute silence and you'll think you have messed up. Then, as a client of mine says, they'll sing like canaries! After a minute or two, turn back and ask who has the first question.

EXERCISE: PRACTISE YOUR TRANSITION TO THE Q&A (5 MINUTES)

1. Decide what to say to cover the three aspects.

2. Practise out loud three times.

3. Add a couple of keywords into your notes to remind you of what you want to say to get questions.

You'll find you get a lot more questions, and that the questions you do get will be of a higher quality. I know this is radical and it takes some guts, but it has never failed to get me questions after a session.

> **!** **WARNING!**
>
> **Questions after the senior pitch**
>
> Use your judgement as to when you use the 'turn to the person next to you' technique. If you're pitching an idea to the board, for example, they probably don't need this to encourage questions. There are no hard-and-fast rules. This technique is more for larger groups who might be reluctant to ask questions.

How to answer questions professionally

I know you're probably familiar with them, but on the safe side, here is the industry best practice on how to answer questions after a presentation.

Industry Standard Presentation Question Answering Best Practice*:

- Let the group know at the start of the Q&A how long you have for questions.

- If you're unsure of the question after it's been asked, feel free to clarify with the questioner.

- If the group is larger than, say, eight or nine people, repeat the question back to the whole group.

- Answer the question to the whole group, not just the questioner.

- Answer briefly, as people can always follow up – 90 seconds is a good rule of thumb.

- If the question is very particular to the questioner's situation, see if you can bring your answer to refer to more general principles that are relevant to the whole group.

* sounds official, huh?

- Before moving on, check with the questioner that you've answered their question sufficiently.

- If you say you'll get back to someone, be sure to get back to them.

- As you're getting to the end of your allotted time, let everyone know.

These guidelines won't necessarily make you shine, but it will make your approach professional.

As the questions start, reward the first and each subsequent one. Consciously or unconsciously, the group will be looking to how you deal with the first person brave enough to stick their hand up. Make sure that you are encouraging with the first questioner, give them your full attention, smile, be warm, maybe ask a small clarification of their question, then answer. In this way, people will understand that asking questions is a good thing.

In general, make sure you follow the best practice outlined above, to include the whole group and keep the questioner happy too.

Practise what to say instead of 'Good question!'

Starting your answer to a question can be tough: you're still thinking about your answer and yet all those people are looking at you. Generally, the first thing you do is to repeat the question back so the whole group can hear it, maybe checking that you've understood it. Then what do you say?

Here are two strategies that can help you get some intelligent words coming out of your mouth.

START WITH A KEYWORD FROM THE QUESTION
Answering a question in front of a group is different to answering an individual in private.

If someone asks you a question in private – such as asking you for your professional opinion in your paid role – you can and should go into all the detail that pertains to their situation.

Answering that same question in a group requires you to keep your attention on the needs of everyone in the room. This means mainly keeping things on the level of general principles applying to the scenario in question. Unless the question is super-simple and quick to answer, stay away from individual details and move the conversation towards the aspects common to everyone listening.

Listen for the main issue in the question. What is the matter at hand?

Start your first sentence with that.

[Keyword/phrase] . . .

[Keyword/phrase] is important because . . .

[Keyword/phrase] has two main aspects . . .

[Keyword/phrase] is a perennial problem . . .

This centres you on the issue, and is an easy sentence for your mind to complete.

EXERCISE: PRACTISE ANSWERING WITH A KEYWORD (20 MINUTES)

1. List a few questions that someone might ask you after your presentation.

2. If you can, get someone to ask you them in a random order. If they can improvise other (pertinent) questions, so much the better!

3. Practise answering, starting the sentence with a keyword from the question.

BEST THING/WORST THING

A slight variation on the keyword method comes from media coach Suzanne Bates. She recommends that when you're totally stuck, say: 'The best thing about [keyword/phrase] is . . . The worst thing about [keyword/phrase] is . . .'

She suggests that your mind can always find the extremes of something. I've never used it myself, but I offer it to you as a technique that might save your brain from freezing one day.

If you do end up saying, 'Good question!', don't beat yourself up about it – just move swiftly to repeating the question and getting to the keyword. It happens!

Next step 1: practise what to say instead of 'I don't know'

When you've been standing up, talking knowledgeably on a topic, it can seem like a nightmare that someone might ask you a question and you have to reply with 'I don't know'.

The best way to avoid getting questions that you can't answer is in how you frame things before the Q&A starts.

Think about your session title

As previously discussed when you initially were planning your presentation, make sure the session title is specific to the level of content that you will be delivering, and that it will attract people with the right level of knowledge. If you've called it: 'Everything you always wanted to know about . . .' or 'Super-Advanced Expert Forum on . . .', you've only got yourself (or your marketing team or boss) to blame.

If you've called it 'Five ways to . . .', or 'Introduction to . . .' or even 'Super-Advanced Expert Forum on [topic you're very familiar with] for [very specific group of people you're very experienced with]', then it's less likely that people will turn up with different expectations of the session to yours.

Practice: can you fix your title?

Think about your session description

If there is a description for your session, make sure you're being accurate about the topics covered, the level that you'll be going into, and specifically who it is and isn't for. Sometimes speakers worry that they won't get enough people coming if they're too specific, so they make the session sound generic and applicable to anyone. The danger here is that they'll get a bunch of people attending who have wildly different needs, which can spell disaster.

Practice: Can you fix your description?

Set boundaries at the beginning of the session

Within the first couple of minutes of your session, say the phrase: 'What I'm not going to be able to do today . . . What I am going to be able to do today . . .'. Let people know what level the session will be at, so the right people relax and the wrong people could even leave if it's not what they expected. If you've been clear about the level and who it's pitched at, you're much less likely to get out-there questions at the wrong level of detail for your knowledge.

What to say if you don't know the answer

Having said all of that, you may still hit situations when you get a question to which you don't know the answer. There are two complementary guiding principles here.

FIND OUT WHAT THE QUESTION ACTUALLY IS

Your first job is to find out what the question is really about. You can do this by using a phrase such as: 'Sorry, can I just check: is your question about [X] or [Y] – or something else?'

Often when you can clarify the scope of the question, you'll discover that there are parts of it that you can answer.

SEPARATE WHAT YOU DO KNOW FROM WHAT YOU DON'T

It's unlikely that you will have absolutely no clue about an answer to a question. (If you do hit that situation, I'll be sharing a magic phrase below which can help you out.)

Here are some ways of approaching this:

> 'I'm not entirely sure of [X]. What I do know is . . .' For example, maybe you don't know how it works in that situation or with that group of people, but you do know how it works in an analogous situation.

> 'Based on what I know about [X], my hunch is that . . .'

> 'I can't tell you [X]. What I can tell you is . . .'

> 'I can answer that in part, but I'll have to get back to you on . . .' – do get back to them, though.

> 'I'm not familiar enough with [X] to even hazard a guess. Let me ask someone and get back to you.' Then get back to them.

> 'That's a little bit specific for this forum. Can I take it up to general principles?' Take it up to a more generic situation that applies to more people in the group.

In general, make sure that your answer helps more people than just that individual. Keep your eye on those outcomes you'd like to happen as a result of your session (e.g. that they approach you afterwards, that they recommend you), and adapt what you're doing with that in mind.

What to do if you really don't know the answer

The secret weapon response if you really can't answer a question is something I learned from a friend. Ask: 'Can you tell me a bit more about what's behind your question?'

The question behind the question is often an answerable one.

If the worst comes to the worst, just say you don't know but you'll find out more and get back to them. However, if you implement what you've learned, that should be a rare occurrence.

**EXERCISE: PRACTICE DEALING WITH 'I DON'T KNOW'
(30 MINUTES)**

1. Check that your title is at the right level.

2. Check your description is at the right level.

3. Practice your boundaries sentence for this presentation out loud three times. Add keywords into your notes as a reminder.

4. Imagine someone asks you a complex question. Practice your 'Is this question about X or Y?' sentence out loud three times.

5. Choose two or three ways for separating what you do know from what you don't know. Practise them out loud three times, so that you are naturally able to produce them in the moment.

6. Practise saying, 'Can you tell me a bit more about your question?' out loud three times.

Next step 2: dealing with a hostile crowd

Of course, now you have all this interaction, you may find that you have some difficult questions to answer!

What to do before presenting to a hostile crowd

How many presentations have you done where people have been actively positive towards your message? How many were to a group who were somewhat hostile? At a conference, it may be that things stay pretty bland, but it's still good to have some strategies to deal with difficult questions before they come up. At least you'll be able to relax, knowing what you might do if things get tense.

Conflict comes from people feeling certain about their point of view.

You can't wait for others to see it your way. In order to change the situation, you have to go there first. If you want to minimise the effects of a conflict situation, see things from their point of view – but genuinely.

If you do, you'll find you're able to structure your communication (and the delivery of your communication) in a way that makes it easier for people to come around to your point of view.

In order for this to work, you have to turn things around in your own head. Here's how.

Work on seeing things from another point of view

REMEMBER WHEN YOU HAVE BEEN MISUNDERSTOOD
To get ready for this work, think of those times when someone has taken something you said the wrong way. For example: they thought you were serious when you were joking; they thought you were furious when you weren't in the slightest; or they thought you were unhappy when you were just distracted.

Notice how often you were oblivious to the problem, and how easily things were sorted out once you knew.

Think of times when you got it wrong, when you thought your colleague was really annoyed with you but they were just busy; or you thought the new guy was snubbing you, when in fact he's shy. You think there's a problem because you sent an email and didn't get a reply when actually it was still in your draft folder, or the person was on holiday, or they'd read it and taken action but forgotten to reply.

Remember how convinced you were that there was a problem, and how surprised you were when you found out the reality.

How about even more basic misunderstandings when things have been misheard, information didn't get through, or you find out that there are bigger factors involved than you knew about.

Human communication is messy. People are involved with a thousand things all at once, both in their working and non-working lives. Misunderstandings happen – a lot.

It's helpful to bear that in mind as you move forward.

FORGET WHAT YOU KNOW
Think about this group of people. If you had only had their experiences, what would you know? What would you suspect? What would you be feeling? This is not a theoretical exercise – take time to truly think about what is going on inside their heads.

GIVE THEM THE BENEFIT OF THE DOUBT
There is often a gap between the intention behind our communication, and the impact that it has. Just for a minute, think about the communication you've received from them. Interpret it in the most positive way that you can. At least momentarily, be compassionate and allow the possibility that what you've taken as hostile or negative might not be.

The flipside of this is to think about what and how *you've* communicated to *them*. What's the most negative way they could have misunderstood you? What might the ramifications be, if this is actually what has happened?

BE WARY OF LABELS
There are no negative people. There are no hostile people. There are only people who've had a set of experiences that have led them to see things in a particular way. Take off the labels and see how much you can empathise with their situation.

WORK OUT WHERE YOU MIGHT ACTUALLY BE WRONG
When going into a negotiation, traditional wisdom says that you should be arriving with strong arguments for 'your' side, ready to pick holes in 'their' side.

I invite you to do exactly the opposite: think about what you consider to be the facts in this situation. Now, thoroughly consider how you might actually be wrong.

For example, they want 99 per cent uptime for their IT system, and you absolutely know that it can't be done with this set-up. How might you be wrong?

They want the project done with half the budget, and you just know that's impossible. How might you be wrong?

Even: you think they want 99 per cent uptime. You think they want the project done with half the budget. Are you sure that's what they want?

DON'T STOP UNTIL YOU FEEL DIFFERENT
Keep going until you think: 'Ah, maybe they do have a point – maybe I am in the wrong here. I can totally see how they've arrived where they are.'

Be careful of 'but'

If you are working to build a connection with people who might not be totally positive towards your message, especially if you're doing that by showing you understand their point of view, be extra careful of one word which can ruin it all for you: 'but'.

THE FUNCTION OF 'BUT'
The function of 'but' is to say, 'What I just said is not true':

'He's a nice guy, but . . .'

'We'd love to give you more budget, but . . .'

'You're doing a good job, but . . .'

– or the one I'm concerned about, when you've been working on seeing their point of view:

'I see your point of view, but . . .'

The 'but' sends a signal that you don't really see things their way. You're merely paying lip service to acknowledging their concerns. It signals that it's time for them to listen to *you* now, thank you very much. It signals that your agreement is insincere, merely a tactic.

If you have really done the work of seeing things from the other person's point of view, you won't use 'but' in that way. You'll be okay with multiple perspectives on the issue, with yours being just one of them.

However, especially as you're getting into the habit of avoiding 'but', there is a game you can play with yourself.

REPLACE 'BUT' WITH 'AND'
Now, I'm not always a fan of replacing one word with another. You can't just replace 'but' with 'however' – 'however' is just a more expensive 'but'.

Saying 'and' instead of 'but' is a bit different, because we're talking about words that perform different functions.

The function of 'but' is to say there are two opposing ideas here.

For example:

> 'I would like to get that report written, *but* I can't find the time.'

(The unspoken thought here is: 'That's the end of the story. I'm not going to write that report, and that's that.')

The function of 'and' is to allow two ideas to coexist:

> 'I would like to get that report written, *and* I can't find the time.'

(Next thought: maybe there are options – I wonder what's in my control?)

So, if you find yourself saying 'I understand your point of view, *but* . . .', you might be able to change that midstream into '*and* . . .' – thus saving the day.

For example:

> 'I know our project's slipping has caused you a lot of trouble in the past [but] *and* I'd like to share a bit about what we've been doing to prevent this happening again.'

(Unspoken thought: 'I see the situation from your point of view, *and* here's some extra data you might not have.')

At least allow your differences to be side-by-side, rather than force them to oppose each other unnecessarily, and perhaps your work on defusing the difficult situation might not go to waste.

> **EXERCISE: PRACTISE REPLACING 'BUT' WITH 'AND' (15 MINUTES)**
>
> 1. Write down your position on a few issues and another opposing position for each one.
>
> 2. Practise saying, 'I know that . . . [view 1] *and* [view 2] . . .'
>
> 3. Reflect on your feelings as you say this. If necessary, spend more time on seeing things genuinely from the other point of view.

Take It Further

Learn more about creating dialogue and dealing with conflict in the Take It Further chapters at:

Andrewlightheart.com/presentationnow

PART 3
EXTEND

Taking your presentation skills into the world means extending your skills beyond traditional circumstances.

This section supports you in:

Conference calls: Speaking in conference calls is a different beast to speaking in a face-to-face environment. This chapter helps you think through how to extend your presentation skills to conference calls. If you worry about how to encourage interaction, this chapter gives you some guidance there too.

Global communication: More and more situations involve extending to speak to people from outside your national culture. Cross-cultural communication is a vast field, and this chapter gives you an accessible starting point.

Confidence: The way you establish your mindset can extend your ability to learn. This chapter gives you a pep talk to read just before a presentation, and something to read just after to make sure you maximise your learning.

12.
Conference calls

Group conference calls are strange. They are taking over our life (at least in the corporate world), yet no one tells us how to deal with them. There are a few things to consider when presenting and creating discussion in a conference call: think about what's missing.

One-to-one, face-to-face conversation

In this kind of conversation, the rules tend to be as follows.

Turn-taking

Only one person talks at once, with minimum overlap. The person listening looks at the person talking. Turns are taken by some culturally acceptable signalling, for example:

- You just start talking and after a moment of overlap, the other person yields their turn.

- You nod quickly and do preparatory gestures such as opening your mouth or taking in an audible breath to show you have something to add, or raising your hands.

Topic

The topic may meander, but it's negotiated reasonably easily by the two parties – non-sequiturs are discouraged or challenged.

Presentations

Presentations in this context are likely to feel more like conversations, perhaps with more discussion than long periods of one-way talking.

One-to-one phone call

A phone call between two people tries to follow the same rules as a face-to-face conversation, but of course it is missing non-verbal signals as to whose turn it is.

Turn-taking

Conversational turn-taking relies on rhythms and intonation for each party to know whether they hold or yield the turn. One place where this becomes complicated is if there is a lag. Face-to-face turn-taking is timed down to the millisecond, with differences determined by which linguistic community you belong to (some communities have more silence between turns, and others overlap more).

Technology such as Skype or even mobile phones demonstrate how finely-tuned the rhythms of conversation are. You stumble and both speak at once and apologise for the lag, and so on. There are culturally agreed politeness rules for how long two people can speak at once before one yields, and when this is interfered with by technology, we get annoyed with how awkward and rude we feel.

In a phone call, you're also missing the non-verbal information from someone's reactions. Are they paying attention or not? Where are they?

That is strange in itself: the fact you can have a conversation and be in two different environments. A question that has only just entered common parlance is: 'Where are you?'

Have you ever asked someone if they were doing something else? (For example, only yesterday I was on the phone to my Nan, and she asked what I was doing. I was in the kitchen, putting away the dishes – oops!) We do things that would be deemed rude in person, but by being invisible we allow ourselves certain permissions. Naturally, the quality of attention you give someone on the phone often has a different intensity than face-to-face.

Topic

A topic in a one-to-one phone call is similar to a one-to-one, face-to-face conversation, in that it is dynamically negotiated between the two people involved.

Presentations

Presentations will feel more conversational, although you are missing the ability to give or receive visual signals.

Face-to-face group meeting

A face-to-face meeting adds an area of complexity to conversational turn-taking.

Turn-taking

The aim for turn-taking in a group conversation is the same as in one-to-one conversation: one person talking at once, with minimum overlap. How we signal whose turn it is to talk becomes more complex.

Formal meeting systems have a chair who should be the 'traffic cop', controlling all turns. While keeping things orderly, it's difficult for conversation to flow this way. If a meeting is to feel more natural, conversational turn-taking happens via non-verbal signals (such as movement, hands raised, small 'Ummm . . . Well . . .' noises), as well as overt requests or demands to take a turn.

A chair who informally signals when it's someone's turn – especially for people who don't feel comfortable taking a turn just by beginning to speak – can be really helpful. Without a skilful chair, the same people in the group are the ones who speak and others stay largely silent.

Topic

Topics may meander, but often are not negotiated with the whole group, resulting in a proportion of the group not participating in a discussion of which they want to be part.

Presentations

Presentations in this context, depending on the size of the group, are more one-way and what we think of as traditional presentations.

Group conference phone calls

With teams being so distributed these days, conference calls are becoming an accepted fact of business life. However, think about what's missing in comparison to two people with similar conversational cultures, speaking face-to-face.

Compare face-to-face conversations with group conference calls

	ONE-TO-ONE, FACE-TO-FACE	GROUP CONFERENCE CALLS
Turn-taking	Only one person talking at once, with minimum overlap.	Turns often significantly overlap or have big silent gaps, due to technology lag.
	The person listening looks at the person talking.	Visual cues are missing. Often listeners don't know who is talking.
	Turns are taken after some type of culturally acceptable signalling.	Natural turn-taking cues are missing.
Topic	The topic may meander, but it's negotiated reasonably easily by the two parties – non-sequiturs are discouraged or challenged.	Participants are often multitasking and can lose track of what the topic is.
Presentations	Presentations in this context are likely to feel more like a conversation, perhaps with more discussion than long periods of one-way information.	Listeners often have technology problems (and are multitasking), making it difficult to track one-way spoken presentations for long.

Turn-taking

Natural turn-taking signals are difficult to manage in a group anyway, but without non-verbal signals it's difficult to know whose turn it is to speak.

LAG
Due to the technology involved, natural conversational rhythms and overlap are impeded.

UNSURE WHO IS SPEAKING
Unlike in one-to-one calls or face-to-face group meetings, no one knows who is speaking. I hear this a lot from people working in large companies: when they are on conference calls with other teams or external people, they don't know who the people are to start with – and even if they do know who is actually on the call, they don't recognise their voices.

TIME ZONES
This is not to be underestimated in global conference calls. Not only are people in different physical environments from each other, but also they will be at different points in their day – or night! For example, my clients in Asia have conference calls at 10, 11 or 12 o'clock at night in order to fit in with the office hours of their colleagues/clients in Europe and the US.

INTIMIDATING SILENCE
If participants are in noisy situations, they will often mute themselves so as not to 'pollute' the call with their ambient noise. It can therefore be intimidating to speak up, as the lack of any kind of audible feedback can be overwhelming.

ATTENTION
Often on conference calls, people are multitasking – that is, they are not focusing totally on the call. For example, a friend of mine used to work for a large multinational company and took conference calls while walking his dog. I've even been round to a friend's house for dinner and he has been on a conference call while eating with us. Every now and again he would have to get up, walk away and urgently unmute! Imagining that people are quietly focused on the matter at hand, as if they are in a face-to-face meeting, is absurd.

So, in summary, it's difficult to know:

- who is in the meeting
- who is speaking
- whose turn it is to speak
- how to take a turn without being rude.

Signals as to whether people are paying attention (or agreeing or disagreeing, etc.) are absent in conference calls, in addition to the fact that it's highly likely that they're not paying full attention at all. Not quite the miracle we were promised.

Presentations

There are a few things to consider when you're planning to present in a conference call. The first thing to do is to go through the planning questions, to make sure you've really thought about who is going to be on the call.

It's also important to remember the exigencies of the situation. Mainly you're thinking about the probability of your outcome. If people are likely not to be paying full attention to you, and the sound quality of the call may be bad (or they may be in a noisy environment, if they're calling in on their mobile), you will have to help them track what you're saying.

EMPHASISE THE BENEFITS OF LISTENING TO YOU
On a conference call you have to work harder to get people's attention. Make it clear what *they* are going to get from listening to you. Return to Planning Question 4 to help you come up with real answers to this. If there are no clear benefits, then you've a hard job on your hands.

MAKE IT CLEAR HOW LONG YOU WILL BE TALKING
Clarity is even more important for conference calls. Give people clear guidelines as to how long you'll be speaking, and what will happen next.

REINFORCE THE BOUNDARIES OF THE SESSION
Be thorough in your 'What's in, what's out' summary at the beginning. The clearer you can be about what you are (and are not) going to cover, the easier it is for people to track what you're saying, and the less likely it will be for conversations to go off track.

MAKE YOUR REQUESTS FOR FEEDBACK CLEAR
What exactly do you need from the people listening? Do you need their reactions and, if so, what specifically? Do you need their overt agreement? Is this the time where you want people to pick holes in the proposal, or are you aiming to get their agreement to a

subsequent interaction (meeting, email, one-to-one phone call)? Do you need to know concerns from their perspective – their region, department, team? Make this clear *before* you begin, then people can listen for that purpose.

USE VISUAL AIDS, PERHAPS WITH WORDS

This is a situation where you may actually need more visual aids. It can be difficult to track what's happening in a presentation where you can't see the speaker (and the speaker can't see you in order to check understanding). So, clear signposting of content is important. If you are speaking a language that other people in the group are less fluent in, or perhaps speak a different version of, then written words can really help them to track what's being discussed. Bear in mind that people might not be able to see visual aids if they're travelling or driving or can't get to their computer, so don't rely on people having these in front of them.

REMEMBER CROSS-CULTURAL ISSUES

Different national cultures use different ways of expressing politeness and turn-taking, so make sure you're taking this into account (for more information on this, see Chapter 13).

SPEAK SLOWLY

It's even more important that you speak slowly and clearly on a conference call. Follow the advice about names of projects, products, people and numbers – say them really clearly. This helps people listening on a poor line, and if your style of speech is different to theirs. Accents are generally much more of a problem if you speak fast, as people won't catch what you're saying. When you slow down and say each word clearly, it's much easier for people to track what you're saying.

SUMMARISE MORE

Even with the best will in the world, people dip in and out of conference calls attention-wise. Someone in their physical environment asks them a question, they check their email, they get dropped off the call. Things happen which mean that constant attention is difficult – even more so than in a face-to-face meeting.

As a result, it's your job as a presenter to summarise much more. Imagine people walking in and out of the meeting, and that you have to keep them up to speed. At each juncture, summarise:

- what's just been discussed
- where you are in the structure of the presentation
- how many points have been discussed
- how many there are to go
- how long there is left of the session.

You have no way of seeing that people are off-track, so you have to assume they *are* off-track and gently bring them back. This will feel like you are over-explaining, but people will feel that you are being clear. Lessening the cognitive load of tracking what is happening allows people to have more of their mind available to focus on your content, recommendations and requests.

Aim to begin a discussion

Listening to long presentations on conference calls is particularly difficult. Even more than normal, think of your presentation as being the beginning of a discussion. You need to think about how to facilitate people speaking up in a group, bearing in mind the features of conference calls we've discussed above.

Good group interaction in conference calls

Make sure you're clear what contributions you want people to make, and when.

If you want discussion during the call that moves people closer to your outcome, encourage two things: focus, and turn-taking.

Focus

The first thing you can do is to be clear what contributions are required. If you want to know whether there are factors or information you've missed out, then ask for those. If you want to know which of three options appeal most, ask. If you want in-depth reality testing down to the commas and the full stops, ask for that (although in reality, a conference call is probably not the best place for that kind of discussion).

Be clear about what interaction is appropriate. If you have three options, let people know you first want input into option one before moving on. However, if you want people's gut reaction to which one of the three seems best, tell them you want them to say A, B or C. Keeping a group on-topic who can't see each other requires you to be very clear about what you want, and when.

If someone seems to go off-topic, it's good practice to ask them how their comment fits with the current theme, rather than tell them they're going off on a tangent.

Turn-taking

Good meetings are where everyone speaks, one at a time. You can let this happen organically, you can set up a system of going 'round the circle', or somewhere in-between. Strange as it might seem when you first do it, asking people directly for their contribution can help everyone feel comfortable.

However, it is good practice to warn people when you're about to come to them. Help people know when it's their turn by saying something like: 'I've got one more point, then I'm going to be asking everyone which option appeals to them and why. Khyati, I'll come to you first, then Immy, then Rahel.' This will allow people to get into a quiet situation, think about their response, get ready to unmute and give their input.

This also requires you to know who's actually on the call. Perfect conference call etiquette would involve people saying their name before they comment, but this takes discipline. You can introduce the idea by saying:

> Sometimes it's hard to keep track of who's speaking in a conference call, so I'm going to say my name every time it's me. I know it feels awkward, but it means everyone is involved and raises the quality of the conversation.

Then do it – every time you're speaking in the conversation part, say your name – for example: 'This is Anneka. I was thinking that maybe . . .'.

Keep remembering the basics (the planning questions, speak slowly, keep breathing), do a thorough reality check on your outcome, and you'll be fine.

SUMMARY

Presenting in a conference call:

Really emphasise the benefits of listening to you.

Make it clear how long you will be talking.

Reinforce the boundaries of the session.

Make your requests clear, particularly for the type of feedback you need.

Use visual aids, perhaps with words.

Remember cross-cultural issues.

Speak slowly.

Summarise more.

Aim to begin a discussion.

Interaction in a conference call:

Create good interaction in a conference call by concentrating on focus and turn-taking.

Take It Further

For up-to-date information on conference calls, including video calls, head to:

andrewlightheart.com/presentationnow

13.
Global communication strategies

Increasingly we are talking to people who are not from our national culture. People from different cultures often speak a different version of the language that we speak, and may have significantly different expectations of presentations and discussion.

The topic of cross-cultural communication is vast, so I'm going to give you some pointers for areas specifically to do with presentations and the subsequent interaction.

Language concerns

In common with many people in the world, I speak English – but really, we all speak many different types of English, for example: Spanish English, British English, Indian English, American English, Hong Kong English. When you're speaking to people who don't speak the same variety of language as you do, it makes for clearer communication if you remember a couple of things.

Use Plain English

There is a lot of chauvinism about 'native English'. The standards that are held up are British English, American English, Australian English, Canadian and New Zealand English. These are the varieties towards which global learners are encouraged to strive. As an active language learner myself, I understand the pressure to 'speak like a native' (let's call these versions 'Anglo English'). A terrible post-colonial heritage creates a structure where those who speak different varieties of English feel looked down upon.

I have lots of clients from across the world, all of whom speak English. Consistently they say that it's easier to understand other non-Anglo speakers of English than it is to understand people from Britain or the United States. One factor that counts towards that is Anglo people unconsciously use non-standard words and phrases.

Having worked with people from tens of different countries, I have had to develop my global English speaking skills. Mainly I am aware of the words I'm using, and make sure that I use plain English, for example: 'ask' rather than 'enquire', 'do' rather than 'implement', 'make' rather than 'fabricate', 'I don't know' instead of 'I am unaware of'. This is not dumbing down, but being clear.

If you go back to the planning questions, remember Planning Question 2: 'What do you want these people to be able and motivated to do as a result of your presentation?' If they haven't been able to understand what you're saying – or have had to work unnecessarily hard to understand it – you're putting barriers in the way of their ability to take the actions you want them to do.

(This is actually good practice anyway, but especially important for global situations.) Go to **andrewlightheart.com/presentationnow** for some additional resources on plain English

Speak really slowly

The more you move out from your 'home' group, the slower you will need to speak. Accents take time for people to tune into, and even if you speak a 'standard' Anglo English dialect, people from other cultures might not have had practice listening to that dialect. If you have ever learned another language, you'll recall how hard it is to keep track of what's going on, how much energy it takes.

Next time you're in a bookshop, go to a section you're unfamiliar with (science, law, something theoretical), open a technical-looking book in the middle and start reading at your normal pace. Keep going until you have to blink and pull your head out.

That is what it feels like when you're listening to someone whose style of language is unfamiliar. It's too late for you to work on changing your accent (although if you speak a non-standard dialect and you do a lot of speaking to global groups, it's not a ridiculous thought); so the best thing you can do to become a clearer global communicator is to slow down. Remember that means to say each word so slowly that you can hear the words you're saying, as you're saying them.

This is also going to help you choose your words more carefully, in order to make sure you're choosing plain English.

Provide written material before a meeting

Speaking to global listeners is one of those special situations where more wordy visual aids might be a good thing. For example, my clients in China find that when they are working with people from the United Kingdom or India, it helps when there are slides for the topics and subtopics being discussed. As before, listeners' curiosity needs to be maintained in balance with feeling safe, but this is one of the few situations in which to err on the side of safety. Extra explanation and extremely clear signposting allow people to keep track of what you're talking about and stay with you.

Interaction concerns

The subject of cross-cultural differences is enormous. National cultures have different:

- levels of expressing emotion
- preferences for physical proximity
- ways of taking and giving turns in conversation
- attitudes to time

– and very different ways of showing respect and politeness.

Do your research

Unless you've lived in another culture or done a lot of travelling (and have read about other cultures), your own national culture can be somewhat invisible to you. It's worth reading a couple of different cross-cultural books that cover the country profiles of some of your participants, so that you can have at least some of the basics down.

Be careful with this country profile information. Before reading about other cultures, pick up the same book and read how they describe your own. Common responses are: 'Well, some of the information is true but only in formal situations, or more for my parents' generation.' Be aware that although mainstream books are rarely totally inaccurate, there are many subtleties in the real world.

Is everyone from your national culture identical? Of course not. Some people are more rambunctious, while others are more quiet and careful. Some are comfortable talking to strangers, while others are more distant. Some people remain formal for longer, while others get familiar more quickly. Any group from the outside seems homogenous, but from the inside has infinite variety. Remember this when you're looking at any national culture from the outside.

Keep your eyes open

Most businesspeople learn something about each other's culture. Both parties make efforts to accommodate the other. One of you has learned to hand your business card over with two hands and use a person's full title, and the other has learned to slap you on the back and call you by a nickname.

It's important to do your research, then stay alert to what's actually happening. Areas to check up on initially are:

- codes of politeness
- conversational turn-taking
- attitudes to time
- physical proximity
- expression of emotion and humour.

SUMMARY: GLOBAL COMMUNICATION STRATEGIES

Language concerns:

Use standard words

Speak really slowly

Provide written material before a meeting

Interaction concerns:

Do your research

Keep your eyes open

Take It Further

For more resources on cross-cultural communication, head to:

andrewlightheart.com/presentationnow

14.
Pep talks

Read this the day before your presentation

At this stage, go back to Chapter 6 and do a reality check. Does your thinking still check out? If so, good. If not, it's not too late for tweaks or, if it comes to it, wholesale change.

Have you got notes that you can use during the presentation?

Have you sorted out any required visual aids that work? Have you produced handouts or takeaways, if needed?

Okay. Now concentrate on keeping your breathing slow and place your attention on what's really happening around you. You are not doing your presentation right now, so any nerves you feel are horror movies. Go back to Chapter 7 if you need to, and revisit the advice about how to calm yourself.

Then just try and get a good night's sleep!

Read this just before your presentation

Right now is another good time to psyche yourself down. You want to feel relaxed, happy, safe and alert. (Well, alert is going to take care of itself, so work on the relaxed, happy and safe part.) Keep your breathing slow, go wide and keep noticing what's actually happening around you. Go for the most vanilla description: 'I can see chairs. I can see walls. I can see people.'

Your preparation is done. You are only in control of what you're going to say, not what they are going to say, do or feel. All you can do is to give it your best shot with the work you have already done. You do not know what is about to happen (remember Find Five, page 97).

What are you going to do immediately after the presentation? Tonight? Tomorrow? Next week? See: you are not going to die!

Keep your breathing slow and your eyes, jaw and shoulders relaxed all the way up to when you begin. See if you can remember that when you glance at your notes.

Good luck!

Read this as soon as you can after your presentation

The main feelings one feels after giving a presentation are disappointment and relief.

The likelihood is that you missed something out. That's normal. Your group probably didn't react quite the way you wanted them to. That's normal. You probably stumbled a bit. That's normal too.

What's important right now is to notice things you did that went okay:

> Did you get some of your points out?
>
> Did you respond to some questions?
>
> Did you link some of your recommendations to benefits?

Noticing what you did well supports you in learning how to keep getting better each time you present, no matter how strongly a part of you wants to criticise.

Read this a few hours after your presentation

Okay, so you survived. Now is the time for a bit of analysis:

> What did you do well in your preparation?
>
> What did you do well in your delivery?
>
> What did you do well in the Q&A?

Make a note. If you could only choose one thing, what would be the thing you'd like to remember to do differently next time? Make a note of that too.

No matter what happened, you learned things. Getting better at presenting is a process – there is no end point. Focus on what you did better as a result of your preparation and structured thinking. Keep it going!

15.
Conclusion

Well done you!

You've planned a presentation that is truly bespoke to the needs of the people listening. You've worked systematically on your skills around calmness, body language, style, storytelling and Q&A. You've already done more than most presenters *ever* do. So be proud of yourself!

The three skills that unlock everything else

Out of everything you've practised, there are three skills that lead to rapid development.

The planning questions

The four planning questions at the beginning of Part 1 of this book are the key to structuring presentations. Most of what you're doing as a speaker is dealing with silent questions and linking your content to benefits. Working through these questions before you think about what you're going to say makes it much easier to be interesting. Practise using them for significant phone calls and meetings, so that they become a habit.

Calm

Adrenaline freezes your brain. Retrain your ability to relax and you'll unlock your access to all your other thinking skills. Plus you'll dial down the drama of planning and delivering presentations. Start with slow breathing.

Speak slowly

When you learn to speak slowly, in addition to the leap in credibility, you'll be able to be more conscious about what to say and how to say it. Things become much more in your control when you say your words slowly and clearly.

What to do now

This can be the beginning of a journey to being a better speaker, if you want. Here are some suggestions as to next steps.

Go through the 'Take It Further' chapters

The 'Take It Further' chapters are designed to help you develop skills that may be beyond your immediate requirements. Register online at **andrewlightheart.com/presentationnow** and work your way through the sections that appeal to you. There are suggestions for other books to read too.

Create a learning log

After each presentation that you do, reflect on what worked. Make a note of it in a place you can return to – it's like sending a message to your future self, saying: 'This worked this time! Do it again!'

If there is something you wish you had done this time, you can put in a reminder about that too. However, you're allowed only *one* challenge for next time per presentation – otherwise it can get overwhelming.

Ignore style, but steal structure

Whenever you're watching another presenter, notice when you get drawn into what they're saying. What did they just do? You could make a cheat sheet of the presentation ingredients in front of you while watching online presentations. Learn how other speakers combine presentation ingredients in ways that get and keep attention, and adapt those recipes for your situation.

Trust yourself

I want presentations to be just one of those things you do every day without any drama, like sending an email or answering the phone. Allow the skills you've developed by following the processes in this book to build your trust in yourself. Presentations don't always go to plan, and they can be hard work – but so can phone calls, meetings and email exchanges. Give presentations as much mental and emotional energy as they require, and no more.

Connect with the real people in front of you, and remember your common humanity.

Make conversational recommendations in your own words, in terms that are relevant to your listeners.

Do it all in your words and your style.

Take a deep breath and realise:

Presentations are something you can do now.

What did you think of this book?

We're really keen to hear from you about this book, so that we can make our publishing even better.

Please log on to the following website and leave us your feedback.

It will only take a few minutes and your thoughts are invaluable to us.

www.pearsoned.co.uk/bookfeedback

Index